WARRIOR REST

*Learning from King David
the Gift of Rest*

John Mabus

Warrior Rest: Learning from King David the Gift of Rest
Copyright © 2012 by John Mabus

ISBN-13: 978-1484923733

ISBN-10: 1484923731

DEDICATION

Over the last two years I have had the profound privilege of working for and with two common men from a special breed of warriors with an uncommon commitment to placing the welfare and security of others before their own, serving with honor on and off the battlefield. These men welcomed me into their community and inspired me to fulfill God's calling on my life among them. Tim and Brit will be a continual example to me of men who have fought the good fight, kept the faith with good a conscience. I will be forever grateful for their leadership and friendship.

John Mabus
11 September 2012

CONTENTS

INTRODUCTION

Over the last years of our country's war efforts, one of the struggles of our warriors and their families is getting times of rest and refreshing sleep. There are many factors that contribute to this reality. Wartime training, operational schedules, traumatic experiences, family life stress, sleeping environments, and even diet can impact a warrior's ability to connect with his Creator's gift of rest and sleep. While military agencies have connected with many in the medical and psychological field to address this problem, I was certain that the Scriptures could also be a resource for warrior rest.

One of the most influential warriors of the biblical tradition is King David. In the Book of Psalms, many of his reflections can be found on his combat and political experiences. Over the course of David's life, he faced various situations that brought on considerable levels of danger, stress, anxiety, and uncertainty. It was in these times that David learned to rest in a relationship with his God.

My prayer is that the reflections found in this short book would encourage warriors and their families toward a relationship with God that follows in the footsteps of David. This book is divided into four chapters that follow a gradual development from wrestling with distress in the night, to gaining perspective, onto praise and into hope for a new morning. While there are several other Psalms not written by David that address rest and sleep (see page 148), I have selected the Psalms of this ancient warrior-king because of his correlating experiences with our contemporary warriors.

HOW TO USE THIS BOOK

Two of the ancient Jewish and Christian disciplines of the spiritual life are solitude and meditation. While the spiritual life is not intended to be lived in independent isolation, personal, private, and prayerful moments are essential for authentic interaction with God. It is in these moments that meditation takes its affective place. While meditation should also be practiced in the context of a faith community, communal reflection is only as good as the individual's willingness to personally wrestle with the implications of a passage of Scripture.

This book is an opportunity to exercise both of these disciplines in order to lead into a resting relationship with God. One possible way to read this book is over the course of four weeks. Choose five days within each of those weeks to review the five psalms of each section. You may use the following method to engage each reflection:

Preparation: As best as you are able, try to get to a private location for personal prayer and meditation. Depending on your personality, this might be in a bedroom, closet, library, park bench, mountain top, office, or chapel. Find a period of time in your day that you choose to set aside other commitments and requirements. Choose a time of day that you will be most alert and able to focus. For some, this might be in the evening hours as a way to reflect and calm yourself after the day's activities, for others it might be early in the morning before the start of the day's activities. Finally, take a moment to ask God to meet with you and to open your mind, heart and life to hear from him through his Word and to know how to find rest in your relationship with Him.

Observation: Each Psalm selection begins with a *Focus Verse.* This is usually one of the verses in the Psalm that speaks specifically to the topic of rest. This passage can serve as a point of meditation- wrestling and intently thinking through its implications. There will be some brief introductory remarks on the Psalm. Next, each Psalm reflection consists of the text of the Psalm from the *New International Version* of the Bible to read. Then there will be a review of the overall structure of the Psalm and key themes. These are all aids for you to observe the passage and its important ideas and concepts.

Interpretation: There will also be a rereading of the Psalm in a different translation of the Psalm from Eugene Peterson's *The Message* Bible. This is a contemporary paraphrase of the Psalm that might help you gain a different perspective of its meaning. Following this reading, there will be some general comments on the key message of the Psalm in regard to rest.

Application: There will be some initial application thoughts to encourage you to go deeper into how David's model might impact your life-either in the season you are in or will be at some time. Also, thinking about people who might be experiencing a similar situation, will allow you to pray for them and understand how this passage might link to contemporary struggles and contexts.

Prayerful Reflection: Finally, there will be a brief prayer of reflection and commitment on the Psalm. This is intended to be a bridge for you into your own prayer. Following the prayer there will be a blank space for writing your own personal reflections, applications and prayers.

DISTRESS IN THE NIGHT

This section of Psalms focuses on David's prayers to God in the midst of great distress and emotional concern. There were many times in David's life that he experienced deep hurt and pain. Two specific times were when King Saul violently hunted him like an outlaw and when his son Absalom rebelled and raised a revolt against him.

When reading these Psalms, you may be able to relate to some of David's emotional expressions to God in the midst of your current struggle. Yet, you might come to them thinking about past experiences or the circumstances of others that are overwhelmed with distress and unable to find rest. Also, becoming familiar with these Psalms will give you a starting place in the future when you don't know where to turn and are distressed and unable to find peace.

You might begin your time reading each of these Psalms by reading or singing one of the two following hymns:

In Need Thee Every Hour-
Words: Annie S. Hawks, 1872.

I need Thee every hour, most gracious Lord;
No tender voice like Thine can peace afford.

I need Thee, O I need Thee;
Every hour I need Thee;
O bless me now, my Savior,
I come to Thee.

I need Thee every hour, stay Thou nearby;
Temptations lose their power when Thou art nigh.

I need Thee, O I need Thee;
Every hour I need Thee;
O bless me now, my Savior,
I come to Thee.

I need Thee every hour, in joy or pain;
Come quickly and abide, or life is in vain.

I need Thee, O I need Thee;
Every hour I need Thee;
O bless me now, my Savior,
I come to Thee.

I need Thee every hour; teach me Thy will;
And Thy rich promises in me fulfill.

I need Thee, O I need Thee;
Every hour I need Thee;
O bless me now, my Savior,
I come to Thee.

Nearer My God to Thee-
Words: Vs 1-2, Sarah F. Adams, 1841; vs 3, Edward H.
Bickersteth, Jr.

Nearer, my God, to thee, nearer to thee!
E'en though it be a cross that raiseth me,
Still all my song shall be, nearer, my God, to Thee.

Nearer, my God, to Thee,
Nearer to Thee!

Though like the wanderer, the sun gone down,
Darkness be over me, my rest a stone.
Yet in my dreams I'd be nearer, my God to Thee.

Nearer, my God, to Thee,
Nearer to Thee!

There in my Father's home, safe and at rest,
There in my Savior's love, perfectly blest;
Age after age to be, nearer my God to Thee.

Nearer, my God, to Thee,
Nearer to Thee!

Psalm 3

Focus Verse:

5 I lie down and sleep;
I wake again, because the LORD sustains me.

David wrote this psalm during one of the most trying times in his reign. In 2 Samuel 15-18, we read about how his son Absalom raised up a rebellion, forcing David out of Jerusalem and into the wilderness of Judah. Eventually, Absalom was killed in battle and David regained his throne.

A psalm of David. When he fled from his son Absalom.
1 LORD, how many are my foes!
How many rise up against me!
2 Many are saying of me,
   "God will not deliver him."

3 But you, LORD, are a shield around me,
   my glory, the One who lifts my head high.
4 I call out to the LORD,
   and he answers me from his holy mountain.

5 I lie down and sleep;
I wake again, because the LORD sustains me.
6 I will not fear though tens of thousands
   assail me on every side.

7 Arise, LORD!
Deliver me, my God!
Strike all my enemies on the jaw;
   break the teeth of the wicked.

[8] From the LORD comes deliverance.
May your blessing be on your people.

David begins by stating the problem up front in specific terms- enemies and naysayers all around (verses 1-2). In the midst these troubles, he starts verses 3-4 with "but", as he turns his mind toward his mighty God who is his defense and the sustainer of his honor. When David is found at a volatile point, David declares that even in his most vulnerable position (sleep) he can find rest in God's sustaining presence (verses 5-6). David makes an honest and direct appeal for God to deal with the injustice around him (verse 7). Finally, David appeals to God's character, asking for His blessing on his people (verse 8).

Take a moment to reread the Psalm in *The Message*.

[1] God! Look! Enemies past counting! Enemies sprouting like mushrooms,
[2] Mobs of them all around me, roaring their mockery: "Hah! No help for him from God!"

[3] But you, God, shield me on all sides;
You ground my feet, you lift my head high;
[4] With all my might I shout up to God, His answers thunder from the holy mountain.

[5] I stretch myself out. I sleep.
Then I'm up again - rested, tall and steady,
[6] Fearless before the enemy mobs coming at me from all sides.

[7] Up, God! My God, help me!
Slap their faces, first this cheek, then the other,

Your fist hard in their teeth!

[8] Real help comes from God. Your blessing clothes your people!

What do we learn from David's words in the Psalm?

First, prayer is specific and honest about the needs and situations we face. We don't do ourselves any good when we are vague to God or ourselves. What troubles us? What is racing through our minds? What keeps us up at night?

Second, like a good conversation, prayer is not static. David doesn't just focus on the enemies, but specifically and intentionally shifts to the character and reputation of God. Our thoughts and prayers take discipline. If you are keeping a journal, this can be done with the turn of a page. Training our minds to shift gears takes time and intentionality, but will help in the path to peace.

Third, our hearts and minds cannot rest when we think we have to stand watch all night over our issues. David shows us that the best investment we can make in helping us deal with tomorrow's issues is a good night's sleep. We can welcome sleep, not as a waste of time but a resupply for the next day's duty.

Prayer:
God, these are the matters that are before me- the challenges, obstacles, enemies, and situations that threaten my peace......... Even though these surround me, I look to you who have been faithful in each generation to hear and sustain your people. Help me tonight to take a deep

breath of dependence on you so that I can rest, refreshed
and ready to face with your help tomorrow's demands.
Amen.

Notes and Personal Prayers:

Psalm 6

⁶ I am worn out from my groaning.
All night long I flood my bed with weeping
    and drench my couch with tears.

This Psalm demonstrates the deep emotional and physical
agony that David experienced at some point in his life
because of his enemy's actions or words. We do not know
what specific event inspired these words. David could
have even written this as a prayer that stayed with him
throughout his many desperate situations.

**For the director of music. With stringed instruments.
According to** *sheminith.* **A psalm of David.**
¹ LORD, do not rebuke me in your anger
    or discipline me in your wrath.
² Have mercy on me, LORD, for I am faint;
    heal me, LORD, for my bones are in agony.
³ My soul is in deep anguish.
    How long, LORD, how long?

⁴ Turn, LORD, and deliver me;
    save me because of your unfailing love.
⁵ Among the dead no one proclaims your name.
    Who praises you from the grave?

⁶ I am worn out from my groaning.
All night long I flood my bed with weeping
    and drench my couch with tears.
⁷ My eyes grow weak with sorrow;
    they fail because of all my foes.

⁸ Away from me, all you who do evil,
   for the LORD has heard my weeping.
⁹ The LORD has heard my cry for mercy;
   the LORD accepts my prayer.
¹⁰ All my enemies will be overwhelmed with shame and anguish;
   they will turn back and suddenly be put to shame.

David declares to God his desperate agony and longing, asking "How long?" he must experience this (verses 1-3). David asks for God's deliverance so he may continue to live a life of worship (verses 4-5). David's foes have robbed him of rest (verses 6-7). David looks forward in expectant faith to God hearing his cry for mercy (verse 8-9).

This Psalm is a clear demonstration that David's combat experience did impact him at a deep level. While David never is recorded to have been wounded in battle, this Psalm demonstrates the mental and emotional wounds that war can cause. These wounds can impact everything from your physical stamina and pain to spiritual perspective.

Take a moment to reread the Psalm in *The Message*.

¹⁻² Please, God, no more yelling, no more trips to the woodshed.
   Treat me nice for a change;
      I'm so starved for affection.

²⁻³ Can't you see I'm black-and-blue,
      beat up badly in bones and soul?
   God, how long will it take

for you to let up?

⁴⁻⁵ Break in, GOD, and break up this fight;
   if you love me at all, get me out of here.
I'm no good to you dead, am I?
   I can't sing in your choir if I'm buried in some tomb!

⁶⁻⁷ I'm tired of all this—so tired. My bed
   has been floating forty days and nights
On the flood of my tears.
   My mattress is soaked, soggy with tears.
The sockets of my eyes are black holes;
   nearly blind, I squint and grope.

⁸⁻⁹ Get out of here, you Devil's crew:
   at last God has heard my sobs.
My requests have all been granted,
   my prayers are answered.

¹⁰ Cowards, my enemies disappear.
   Disgraced, they turn tail and run.

While this Psalm is one of David's shorter Psalms and does not have a specific event in mind, it is a great grace from God because it invites us to bring to it our own situation. Here are a few things that it invites us to consider.

First, when we are in a place like he describes- faint, agony, anguish, worn out, groaning, weeping, and weak with sorrow- how does it impact our relationship with God? David felt like God was possibly angry with him, disciplining him with his wrath. This is a very common reaction in times of anguish and grief. The impacts of combat- trauma, death, loss of limbs and emotional and moral scares can at times make us doubt God's favor toward us and timing. David is open about these feelings, yet he looks to God's unfailing love to guide him through this. How about us? There may be times that you don't feel God's unfailing love or wonder how long you must hold on. David gives us an example of what it looks like to look forward in faith. He calls us to entrust our situation to God's attentive, intervening and unfailing love and mercy.

Second, the intense experience that David has is not just kept in his head. His strength is faint and worn out because of it. He says that his bones are actually in agonizing pain. His eyes are weakened and failing. We cannot mask forever the impact of wounds that we have because of some traumatic experience or the continual exposure to intense and straining demands. This Psalm challenges us to recognize the physical impact of stress. Yet, David like a good warrior is not content to stay there. He asks God to transfer this experience to his enemies. How about us? How have you been impacted physically by the stress you have or are facing? What has helped you pull through this? Have you sought God's aid and the godly wisdom from others?

Prayer:
Yahweh, you are the God how hears and answers the cry of your servants. I confess to you that the situations I face are beyond my ability to maintain. I am confused about you, myself and others. Help me to trust and know your unfailing love when I feel like my faith is failing. Amen.

Notes and Personal Prayers:

Psalm 22

2 My God, I cry out by day, but you do not answer,
    by night, but I find no rest.

David writes this Psalm at a time when he had felt
abandoned by God and scorned by everyone else. This is
also the Psalm that Jesus quoted while hanging on the
cross.

**For the director of music. To the tune of "The Doe of the
Morning." A psalm of David.**
1 My God, my God, why have you forsaken me?
    Why are you so far from saving me,
    so far from my cries of anguish?
2 My God, I cry out by day, but you do not answer,
    by night, but I find no rest.

3 Yet you are enthroned as the Holy One;
    you are the one Israel praises.
4 In you our ancestors put their trust;
    they trusted and you delivered them.
5 To you they cried out and were saved;
    in you they trusted and were not put to shame.

6 But I am a worm and not a man,
    scorned by everyone, despised by the people.
7 All who see me mock me;
    they hurl insults, shaking their heads.
8 "He trusts in the LORD," they say,
    "let the LORD rescue him.
Let him deliver him,
    since he delights in him."

⁹ Yet you brought me out of the womb;
   you made me trust in you, even at my mother's breast.
¹⁰ From birth I was cast on you;
   from my mother's womb you have been my God.

¹¹ Do not be far from me,
   for trouble is near
   and there is no one to help.

¹² Many bulls surround me;
   strong bulls of Bashan encircle me.
¹³ Roaring lions that tear their prey
   open their mouths wide against me.
¹⁴ I am poured out like water,
   and all my bones are out of joint.
My heart has turned to wax;
   it has melted within me.
¹⁵ My mouth is dried up like a potsherd,
   and my tongue sticks to the roof of my mouth;
   you lay me in the dust of death.

¹⁶ Dogs surround me,
   a pack of villains encircles me;
   they pierce my hands and my feet.
¹⁷ All my bones are on display;
   people stare and gloat over me.
¹⁸ They divide my clothes among them
   and cast lots for my garment.

¹⁹ But you, LORD, do not be far from me.
   You are my strength; come quickly to help me.
²⁰ Deliver me from the sword,
   my precious life from the power of the dogs.

²¹ Rescue me from the mouth of the lions;
   save me from the horns of the wild oxen.

²² I will declare your name to my people;
   in the assembly I will praise you.
²³ You who fear the LORD, praise him!
   All you descendants of Jacob, honor him!
   Revere him, all you descendants of Israel!
²⁴ For he has not despised or scorned
   the suffering of the afflicted one;
he has not hidden his face from him
   but has listened to his cry for help.

²⁵ From you comes the theme of my praise in the great
assembly;
   before those who fear you I will fulfill my vows.
²⁶ The poor will eat and be satisfied;
   those who seek the LORD will praise him—
   may your hearts live forever!

²⁷ All the ends of the earth
   will remember and turn to the LORD,
and all the families of the nations
   will bow down before him,
²⁸ for dominion belongs to the LORD
   and he rules over the nations.

²⁹ All the rich of the earth will feast and worship;
   all who go down to the dust will kneel before him—
   those who cannot keep themselves alive.
³⁰ Posterity will serve him;
   future generations will be told about the Lord.
³¹ They will proclaim his righteousness,

declaring to a people yet unborn:
He has done it!

David begins by describing how he cannot find rest because he feels forsaken by God (verses 1-2). He leans into the heritage of his people who have trusted God for centuries (verses 3-5). While David is despised, mocked and degraded (verses 6-8), he grounds himself in God's all knowing care from his birth (verses 9-10). The heart of David's prayer is for God's help and presence when he has been abandoned (verse 11). The beastly threats of his enemies melt his strength (verses 12-15) and ravage his dignity (verses 16-18). David confidently trusts in God's strength (verses 19-21), pledges his praise to God and calls others to worship (verses 22-24). David seeks God's deliverance in this time of need (verse 25-26), and God's honor among the nations (verses 27-29) and generations (verses 29-31) through his acts of help.

This Psalm is one of the clear expressions of David wrestling with distress into the night hours. He tells us that night and day he has been overwhelmed with anguish while he cried out to God. David found that his feelings of abandonment by God and the public scorn shook him all hours of the day.

Take a moment to reread the Psalm in *The Message*.

1-2 God, God...my God! Why did you dump me
    miles from nowhere?
  Doubled up with pain, I call to God
    all the day long. No answer. Nothing.
  I keep at it all night, tossing and turning.

3-5 And you! Are you indifferent, above it all,
    leaning back on the cushions of Israel's praise?
We know you were there for our parents:
    they cried for your help and you gave it;
    they trusted and lived a good life.

6-8 And here I am, a nothing—an earthworm,
    something to step on, to squash.
Everyone pokes fun at me;
    they make faces at me, they shake their heads:
"Let's see how God handles this one;
    since God likes him so much, let him help him!"

9-11 And to think you were midwife at my birth,
    setting me at my mother's breasts!
When I left the womb you cradled me;
    since the moment of birth you've been my God.
Then you moved far away
    and trouble moved in next door.
I need a neighbor.

12-13 Herds of bulls come at me,
    the raging bulls stampede,
Horns lowered, nostrils flaring,
    like a herd of buffalo on the move.

14-15 I'm a bucket kicked over and spilled,
    every joint in my body has been pulled apart.
My heart is a blob
    of melted wax in my gut.
I'm dry as a bone,
    my tongue black and swollen.
They have laid me out for burial
    in the dirt.

¹⁶⁻¹⁸ Now packs of wild dogs come at me;
   thugs gang up on me.
They pin me down hand and foot,
   and lock me in a cage—a bag
Of bones in a cage, stared at
   by every passerby.
They take my wallet and the shirt off my back,
   and then throw dice for my clothes.

¹⁹⁻²¹ You, GOD—don't put off my rescue!
   Hurry and help me!
Don't let them cut my throat;
   don't let those mongrels devour me.
If you don't show up soon,
   I'm done for—gored by the bulls,
   meat for the lions.

²²⁻²⁴ Here's the story I'll tell my friends when they come to
worship,
   and punctuate it with Hallelujahs:
Shout Hallelujah, you God-worshipers;
   give glory, you sons of Jacob;
   adore him, you daughters of Israel.
He has never let you down,
   never looked the other way
   when you were being kicked around.
He has never wandered off to do his own thing;
   he has been right there, listening.

²⁵⁻²⁶ Here in this great gathering for worship
   I have discovered this praise-life.
And I'll do what I promised right here
   in front of the God-worshipers.

Down-and-outers sit at GOD's table
   and eat their fill.
Everyone on the hunt for God
   is here, praising him.
"Live it up, from head to toe.
   Don't ever quit!"

27-28 From the four corners of the earth
   people are coming to their senses,
   are running back to GOD.
Long-lost families
   are falling on their faces before him.
GOD has taken charge;
   from now on he has the last word.

29 All the power-mongers are before him
   —worshiping!
All the poor and powerless, too
   —worshiping!
Along with those who never got it together
   —worshiping!

30-31 Our children and their children
   will get in on this
As the word is passed along
   from parent to child.
Babies not yet conceived
   will hear the good news—
   that God does what he says.

When we face thoughts of abandonment and hopelessness
that run uncontrolled through our minds, David provides
wisdom. Look at how he brings these thoughts and
emotions into perspective and control. He is clear with

how he feels, yet he looks back to those who have gone before him for encouragement. We too can take time to connect with stories from the past. We can do this through reading biographies and listening to stories of past generations. There is much that can help our uncontrolled thoughts by learning from the past and how others trusted in God. David also recounts how God has been with him since birth. It is the past experiences of his ancestors and himself that help ground his thinking and renew his petition.

As the Psalm develops, we see that David is struck again by demoralizing threats. He reaches out for God's rescue and strength. Instead of revisiting his fears, he moves to how he and generations and nations will honor God's faithful care of his people. This Psalm points us to a healthy rhythm of dealing with the thoughts that threaten to rob us of peace and rest (past lessons; present praise; future perspective). Jesus went to this Psalm and pattern while he was fighting the hardest warfare against sin, evil and death on the cross. We can look at the pattern of David's petitions, perspectives and praises as a guide for our own concerns.

Prayer:
Holy One, while I am surrounded by trouble, doubt and anguish, I look to you who stand enthroned above it all. I entrust my circumstances into your justice and rescue. Through it all, help me to trust you, honor you and encourage future generations and even the nations to worship you for your great faithfulness. Amen.

Notes and Personal Prayers:

Psalm 32

Focus Verse:
[4] For day and night
your hand was heavy on me;
my strength was sapped
as in the heat of summer.

David writes this Psalm to encourage repentance and call others through his testimony to get right with God. One of the major events in David's life that he sought forgiveness for was his adultery with Bathsheba and murdered her husband (2 Samuel 11-12).

Of David. A *maskil*.
[1] Blessed is the one
whose transgressions are forgiven,
whose sins are covered.
[2] Blessed is the one
whose sin the LORD does not count against them
and in whose spirit is no deceit.

[3] When I kept silent,
my bones wasted away
through my groaning all day long.
[4] For day and night
your hand was heavy on me;
my strength was sapped
as in the heat of summer.

[5] Then I acknowledged my sin to you
and did not cover up my iniquity.
I said, "I will confess
my transgressions to the LORD."

And you forgave
  the guilt of my sin.

⁶ Therefore let all the faithful pray to you
  while you may be found;
surely the rising of the mighty waters
  will not reach them.
⁷ You are my hiding place;
  you will protect me from trouble
  and surround me with songs of deliverance.

⁸ I will instruct you and teach you
in the way you should go;
  I will counsel you with my loving eye on you.
⁹ Do not be like the horse or the mule,
  which have no understanding
but must be controlled by bit and bridle
  or they will not come to you.
¹⁰ Many are the woes of the wicked,
  but the LORD's unfailing love
  surrounds the one who trusts in him.

¹¹ Rejoice in the LORD and be glad, you righteous;
  sing, all you who are upright in heart!

David proclaims that those who are reconciled with God
find true blessing (verses 1-2). He describes the heavy
conviction of God that stayed with him day and night
(verses 3-4). He specifically remembers how he sought
forgiveness for his deeds (verse 5). David encourages all
to find refuge in God's mercy (verses 8-10). On the others
side of forgiveness, David calls for songs of joy and
gladness (verse 11).

What does real courage look like? Often we limit courage to the battlefield. Yet, David also learned courage off the battlefield that probably gave him greater focus and purpose even in combat. It was courageous honesty and repentance before God. David says that there is renewed blessing and joy for those who have forgiveness from their Heavenly Father. The intense pressure that unresolved sin can cause can greatly impact a person- both physically and spiritually. Our broken relationship with God and our rebellious independence take us away from the true source of life- we waste away, groan and are sapped of strength and resolve.

Take a moment to reread the Psalm in *The Message*.

[1] Count yourself lucky, how happy you must be—
you get a fresh start,
    your slate's wiped clean.

[2] Count yourself lucky—
    GOD holds nothing against you
    and you're holding nothing back from him.

[3] When I kept it all inside,
    my bones turned to powder,
    my words became daylong groans.

[4] The pressure never let up;
    all the juices of my life dried up.

[5] Then I let it all out;
    I said, "I'll make a clean breast of my failures to GOD."
  Suddenly the pressure was gone—
    my guilt dissolved,

my sin disappeared.

⁶ These things add up. Every one of us needs to pray;
   when all hell breaks loose and the dam bursts
   we'll be on high ground, untouched.

⁷ GOD's my island hideaway,
   keeps danger far from the shore,
   throws garlands of hosannas around my neck.

⁸ Let me give you some good advice;
   I'm looking you in the eye
   and giving it to you straight:

⁹ "Don't be ornery like a horse or mule
   that needs bit and bridle
   to stay on track."

¹⁰ God-defiers are always in trouble;
   GOD-affirmers find themselves loved
   every time they turn around.

¹¹ Celebrate GOD.
   Sing together—everyone!
   All you honest hearts, raise the roof!

The ravages of combat and war can sometimes put a
heavy weight upon us that injures our sense of truth and
justice. Sometimes this is caused by the enemy, a comrade
or even by our own regrettable actions. One of the
greatest and healing gifts God gives us is the opportunity
to acknowledge sin. We don't have to cover it up but can
confess it and seek forgiveness. We can also then extend it
to another if needed.

One of the great warrior traditions is to make your "peace with your Maker" before an intense conflict. Yet, there might be a deeper and more life changing impact when our relationship with God is reconciled at the close of each day. Before we put our head on our pillow, we could put our knees on the floor and confess our sins and the sins of others, seeking forgiveness and reconciliation. As we prepare for sleep, we can then embrace the blessing of God's unfailing love as we entrust ourselves to his mercy.

Prayer:
Merciful God, I know that sin- mine especially- has robed me of life and true relationship with you and others. I acknowledge my rebellion and destructive decisions that have weighed me down and separated me from you. Help me to pursue reconciliation with those I have hurt and who have hurt me. Heal me from my stubborn pride and help me to follow your way and walk in your forgiveness. Amen.

Notes and Personal Prayers:

Psalm 55

[17] Evening, morning and noon
   I cry out in distress,
   and he hears my voice.

In this Psalm, David shows us that deep emotional pain
can overwhelm us and cause us to feel like death has
swallowed us up. This emotional pain can be even worse
when the cause is from betrayal. David was overwhelmed
not just from the dangers of an enemy's threat but by a
friend's destructive lies.

**For the director of music. With stringed instruments.
A *maskil* of David.**

[1] Listen to my prayer, O God,
   do not ignore my plea;
[2]   hear me and answer me.
My thoughts trouble me and I am distraught
[3]   because of what my enemy is saying,
   because of the threats of the wicked;
for they bring down suffering on me
   and assail me in their anger.

[4] My heart is in anguish within me;
   the terrors of death have fallen on me.
[5] Fear and trembling have beset me;
   horror has overwhelmed me.
[6] I said, "Oh, that I had the wings of a dove!
   I would fly away and be at rest.
[7] I would flee far away
   and stay in the desert;
[8] I would hurry to my place of shelter,
   far from the tempest and storm. "

⁹ Lord, confuse the wicked, confound their words,
  for I see violence and strife in the city.
¹⁰ Day and night they prowl about on its walls;
  malice and abuse are within it.
¹¹ Destructive forces are at work in the city;
  threats and lies never leave its streets.

¹² If an enemy were insulting me,
  I could endure it;
if a foe were rising against me,
  I could hide.
¹³ But it is you, a man like myself,
  my companion, my close friend,
¹⁴ with whom I once enjoyed sweet fellowship
  at the house of God,
as we walked about
  among the worshipers.

¹⁵ Let death take my enemies by surprise;
  let them go down alive to the realm of the dead,
  for evil finds lodging among them.

¹⁶ As for me, I call to God,
  and the LORD saves me.
¹⁷ Evening, morning and noon
  I cry out in distress,
  and he hears my voice.
¹⁸ He rescues me unharmed
  from the battle waged against me,
  even though many oppose me.
¹⁹ God, who is enthroned from of old,
  who does not change—

he will hear them and humble them,
  because they have no fear of God.

[20] My companion attacks his friends;
  he violates his covenant.
[21] His talk is smooth as butter,
  yet war is in his heart;
his words are more soothing than oil,
  yet they are drawn swords.

[22] Cast your cares on the LORD
  and he will sustain you;
he will never let
  the righteous be shaken.
[23] But you, God, will bring down the wicked
  into the pit of decay;
the bloodthirsty and deceitful
  will not live out half their days.

But as for me, I trust in you.

David begins by seeking God's attention while his
thoughts are overwhelming him (verse 1-3). In verses 4-8,
he describes the extreme emotional impact and his desire
for God's shelter. David petitions God to thwart his
stalkers' abuse (verses 9-11). This threat is coming from
one who he used to be very close (verses 12-14). David
asks God to bring back on them what they are doing to
him (verse 15). In the midst of this distress, David
demonstrates his ongoing trust and dependence on God's
faithful care (verses 16-19). Again, David describes the
attack and deception of his friend (verse 20-21). In verse
22-23, David looks outward to encourage the people of

God to cast their cares to God's faithful care. Finally,
David ends with an affirmation of trust in God (verse 23b.)

Take a moment to reread the psalm in *The Message*.

1-3 Open your ears, God, to my prayer;
   don't pretend you don't hear me knocking.
Come close and whisper your answer.
   I really need you.
I shudder at the mean voice,
   quail before the evil eye,
As they pile on the guilt,
   stockpile angry slander.

4-8 My insides are turned inside out;
   specters of death have me down.
I shake with fear,
   I shudder from head to foot.
"Who will give me wings," I ask—
   "wings like a dove?"
Get me out of here on dove wings;
   I want some peace and quiet.
I want a walk in the country,
   I want a cabin in the woods.
I'm desperate for a change
   from rage and stormy weather.

9-11 Come down hard, Lord—slit their tongues.
   I'm appalled how they've split the city
Into rival gangs
   prowling the alleys
Day and night spoiling for a fight,
   trash piled in the streets,
Even shopkeepers gouging and cheating

in broad daylight.

12-14 This isn't the neighborhood bully
    mocking me—I could take that.
This isn't a foreign devil spitting
    invective—I could tune that out.
It's you! We grew up together!
    You! My best friend!
Those long hours of leisure as we walked
    arm in arm, God a third party to our conversation.

15 Haul my betrayers off alive to hell—let them
    experience the horror, let them
    feel every desolate detail of a damned life.

16-19 I call to God;
    GOD will help me.
At dusk, dawn, and noon I sigh
    deep sighs—he hears, he rescues.
My life is well and whole, secure
    in the middle of danger
Even while thousands
    are lined up against me.
God hears it all, and from his judge's bench
    puts them in their place.
But, set in their ways, they won't change;
    they pay him no mind.

20-21 And this, my best friend, betrayed his best friends;
    his life betrayed his word.
All my life I've been charmed by his speech,
    never dreaming he'd turn on me.
His words, which were music to my ears,
    turned to daggers in my heart.

[22-23] Pile your troubles on GOD's shoulders—
    he'll carry your load, he'll help you out.
  He'll never let good people
    topple into ruin.
  But you, God, will throw the others
    into a muddy bog,
  Cut the lifespan of assassins
    and traitors in half.
  And I trust in you.

How do we wrestle with the deep emotional pain and the cares that cause us anguish? David is not one to sugarcoat or be insincere about his emotions. His method of making it through the tempest and storm is to call out, to plea, to cry out to the One who is enthroned from of old. This is not a onetime emotional breakdown. The threat is constant, even through the night watches. He raises his cry, evening, morning and noon. This may be actually referring to regularly set periods of prayer or it may be a poetic way of saying, "All the time, throughout the day, I am letting God know what I am struggling with."

David is consistent and honest about his emotional weight. He is also honest about his desire for God to deal decisively with the evil that is threatening. David trusts God and casts his cares, laying them into God's hands, believing that God will sustain him.

If before bed is the only time we wrestle with our emotions and seek God's quick fix, we will find it difficult to really rest in God's care. Instead, as we walk through the day, there may be set times, one being before bed but other times too that we can cultivate an honest dialogue with God Throughout our working, walking and relating, we can cast our cares into God's power and control.

Forgiveness and forbearing with emotional pain caused by others takes great emotional intentionality. Sometimes minute-to-minute we have to surrender the person or situation to God's mercy or justice. Our prayers of surrender may have to be often certain days. As we let him know our fears and our trembling, we can move into the shelter of his rest.

Prayer:
Yahweh, these are my emotions……. These are the relationships that experience brokenness, disappointment and strain…….. I give you these situations and cares and ask for you to intervene. Sustain me in the midst of the storms. In the night, may I find help for the battle that rages around and inside me. Amen.

Notes and Personal Prayers:

PERSPECTIVE IN THE NIGHT

This section of Psalms focuses on where David finds perspective to help him through the night and bring him into God's rest. David was not a perfect man and regularly called himself back to God's word and to wise and godly people to help him stay on the right course when things were confusing and overwhelming. .

When reading these Psalms, it might be helpful to note the specific ways that David gains perspective and see if they could be applied to your own life. Possibly, you may know someone who is struggling to find purpose and perspective. You might be able to use these Psalms as a source of prayer and encouragement for them too.

You might begin your time reading each of these Psalms by reading or singing one of the two following hymns:

Our God, Our Help In Ages Past
Words: Isaac Watts, 1719.

Our God, our help in ages past,
Our hope for years to come,
Our shelter from the stormy blast,
And our eternal home.

Under the shadow of Thy throne
Thy saints have dwelt secure;
Sufficient is Thine arm alone,
And our defense is sure.

Before the hills in order stood,
Or earth received her frame,
From everlasting Thou art God,
To endless years the same.

A thousand ages in Thy sight
Are like an evening gone;
Short as the watch that ends the night
Before the rising sun.

Our God, our help in ages past,
Our hope for years to come,
Be Thou our guard while troubles last,
And our eternal home.

He Leadeth Me
Words: Joseph H. Gilmore, 1862.

He leadeth me, O blessed thought!
O words with heav'nly comfort fraught!
Whate'er I do, where'er I be
Still 'tis God's hand that leadeth me.

He leadeth me, He leadeth me,
By His own hand He leadeth me;
His faithful follower I would be,
For by His hand He leadeth me.

Sometimes mid scenes of deepest gloom,
Sometimes where Eden's bowers bloom,
By waters still, over troubled sea,
Still 'tis His hand that leadeth me.

He leadeth me, He leadeth me,
By His own hand He leadeth me;
His faithful follower I would be,
For by His hand He leadeth me.

Lord, I would place my hand in Thine,
Nor ever murmur nor repine;
Content, whatever lot I see,
Since 'tis my God that leadeth me.

He leadeth me, He leadeth me,
By His own hand He leadeth me;
His faithful follower I would be,
For by His hand He leadeth me.

Psalm 4

Focus Verse:
[8] In peace I will lie down and sleep,
for you alone, LORD,
make me dwell in safety.

While we don't know exactly when David wrote this
Psalm, it could have been in the same context of Psalm 3-
the revolt of his son Absalom and the ensuing civil war.
We do know that it was a time of great distress, when his
calling and personal and public honor where being
questioned by his enemies.

**For the director of music. With stringed instruments.
A psalm of David.**
[1] Answer me when I call to you,
 my righteous God.
Give me relief from my distress;
 have mercy on me and hear my prayer.

[2] How long will you people turn my glory into shame?
 How long will you love delusions and seek false gods?
[3] Know that the LORD has set apart his faithful servant for
himself;
 the LORD hears when I call to him.

[4] Tremble and do not sin;
 when you are on your beds,
 search your hearts and be silent.
[5] Offer the sacrifices of the righteous
 and trust in the LORD.

[6] Many, LORD, are asking, "Who will bring us prosperity?"
 Let the light of your face shine on us.

[7] Fill my heart with joy
   when their grain and new wine abound.

[8] In peace I will lie down and sleep,
   for you alone, LORD,
   make me dwell in safety.

David begins this psalm with a cry to God to hear and
answer him (verse 1). In verses 2-3, David speaks to his
slanderers, questioning their destructive ambitions and
reminding them of God's loyalty to him as the chosen
king. David challenges his enemies to use their night time
plotting to turn their hearts to God and away from sin
(verses 4-5). In the midst of this conflict, David's followers
were beginning to doubt God's plan and provision for
them, but David looks with confidence to God for his
blessing (verse 6-7). It is with this confidence that he can
lay down and sleep in safety, entrusted to God's watch.

Take a moment to reread the Psalm in *The Message*.

[1] When I call, give me answers.
God, take my side! Once, in a tight place,
you gave me room;
Now I'm in trouble again: grace me! hear me!

[2] You rabble - how long do I put up with your scorn?
How long will you lust after lies?
How long will you live crazed by illusion?
[3] Look at this: look who got picked by God!
He listens the split second I call to him.

[4] Complain if you must, but don't lash out.
Keep your mouth shut, and let your heart do the talking.

⁵ Build your case before God and wait for his verdict.

⁶ Why is everyone hungry for more?
"More, more," they say. "More, more."
I have God's more-than-enough,
⁷ More joy in one ordinary day than they get in all their shopping sprees.

⁸ At day's end I'm ready for sound sleep,
For you, God, have put my life back together.

What do we learn from David's words in the Psalm? First, David shows us that we do not bring the concerns of our day to a distant, irrelevant or distracted higher power. No, he says "my righteous God." David knew personally, that God had an intervening track record to stick up for what is right, true and just. Do we know God as our God, who we can entrust our distress?

Second, David brings before God the conversations that are running through his head. Often, we let the words of others or the words we want to say to others run through our minds uncontrolled. These conversations don't have to run unchecked through our thoughts. They can and should be brought to God, asking him for wisdom, intervention and transformation in those relationships and situations.

Third, a deep delight and joy in God himself, not our circumstances can keep us from letting our circumstances rock us back and forth. True rest and real sleep do not come just through technique, but a frame of mind and a grounded and glad-hearted relationship with our Creator who holds our times in his hands.

Prayer:
God you are the only one who does not change and who can be counted on to bring true justice. I choose joy in a relationship with you, not a fragile happiness based off shifting circumstances or imperfect people. I entrust to you the conversations that run through my head today. I choose to physically demonstrate my trust and reliance on you by lying down and sleeping in your protective presence. Amen.

Notes and Personal Prayers:

Psalm 19

Focus Verse:

[1] The heavens declare the glory of God;
the skies proclaim the work of his hands.
[2] Day after day they pour forth speech;
night after night they reveal knowledge.

David often writes about the glory of God's creation, both in the created order and in God's Word. In this Psalm, he reminds us of the value they both have to communicate truth.

For the director of music. A psalm of David.

[1] The heavens declare the glory of God;
the skies proclaim the work of his hands.
[2] Day after day they pour forth speech;
night after night they reveal knowledge.
[3] They have no speech, they use no words;
no sound is heard from them.
[4] Yet their voice goes out into all the earth,
their words to the ends of the world.
In the heavens God has pitched a tent for the sun.
[5]   It is like a bridegroom coming out of his chamber,
like a champion rejoicing to run his course.
[6] It rises at one end of the heavens
and makes its circuit to the other;
nothing is deprived of its warmth.

[7] The law of the LORD is perfect,
refreshing the soul.
The statutes of the LORD are trustworthy,
making wise the simple.
[8] The precepts of the LORD are right,
giving joy to the heart.

The commands of the LORD are radiant,
    giving light to the eyes.
9 The fear of the LORD is pure,
    enduring forever.
The decrees of the LORD are firm,
    and all of them are righteous.

10 They are more precious than gold,
    than much pure gold;
they are sweeter than honey,
    than honey from the honeycomb.
11 By them your servant is warned;
    in keeping them there is great reward.
12 But who can discern their own errors?
    Forgive my hidden faults.
13 Keep your servant also from willful sins;
    may they not rule over me.
Then I will be blameless,
    innocent of great transgression.

14 May these words of my mouth
and this meditation of my heart
    be pleasing in your sight,
    LORD, my Rock and my Redeemer.

David celebrates how the heavenly bodies declare God's glory (verses 1-6). He reflects on the life transforming power of God's words (verses 7-9). He prays that his life would live in faithfulness to these words (verses 10-13). David concludes by asking God to help him make his own words in his heart and from his mouth bring glory to God (verse 14).

At the end of the day, there are often many words that run through our minds and on our hearts. Often, these words come from others' actual or perceived opinions or appraisals of us. These words may come from good sources like encouraging words from a friend. The words we have spoken, want to speak, or have to speak also may race through our minds.

Take a moment to reread the psalm in *The Message*.

1-2 God's glory is on tour in the skies,
God-craft on exhibit across the horizon.
   Madame Day holds classes every morning,
      Professor Night lectures each evening.

3-4 Their words aren't heard,
     their voices aren't recorded,
  But their silence fills the earth:
     unspoken truth is spoken everywhere.

4-5 God makes a huge dome
     for the sun—a superdome!
  The morning sun's a new husband
     leaping from his honeymoon bed,
  The daybreaking sun an athlete
     racing to the tape.

6 That's how God's Word vaults across the skies
     from sunrise to sunset,
  Melting ice, scorching deserts,
     warming hearts to faith.

7-9 The revelation of GOD is whole
     and pulls our lives together.

The signposts of GOD are clear
   and point out the right road.
The life-maps of GOD are right,
   showing the way to joy.
The directions of GOD are plain
   and easy on the eyes.
GOD's reputation is twenty-four-carat gold,
   with a lifetime guarantee.
The decisions of GOD are accurate
   down to the nth degree.

[10] God's Word is better than a diamond,
   better than a diamond set between emeralds.
You'll like it better than strawberries in spring,
   better than red, ripe strawberries.

[11-14] There's more: God's Word warns us of danger
   and directs us to hidden treasure.
Otherwise how will we find our way?
   Or know when we play the fool?
Clean the slate, God, so we can start the day fresh!
   Keep me from stupid sins,
   from thinking I can take over your work;
Then I can start this day sun-washed,
   scrubbed clean of the grime of sin.
These are the words in my mouth;
   these are what I chew on and pray.
Accept them when I place them
   on the morning altar,
O God, my Altar-Rock,
   God, Priest-of-My-Altar.

David challenges us to examine the words that go through
our thoughts. Creation, while not using human words,

communicates the wonder and glory of God- day and night (some would say even more in the night sky). The Scriptures are filled with God's refreshing, wise, joyful, revealing, enduring and right words about who He is, who we are, and what this world is all about.

David encourages us to bind our lives to these types of words. He warns us to avoid words that enslave us to destructive thoughts and unwise actions. He demonstrates for us an open heart before God- his Rock and Redeemer. As we approach resting in God's presence, it is so important to check our thoughts for error and for that which glorifies God and honors his work in our lives and history.

Before resting, look at David's example. Take in the night sky and the beauty of God's creation. Meditate and guide your thoughts with the Scriptures- God's perfect, trustworthy, right, radiant, pure and firm words. Think on them; speak them; live them.

Prayer:
God who speaks good and life giving words, search me- the words of my mouth, in my mind and lived with my actions. May all of my life bring you glory and honor your character. Amen.

Notes and Personal Prayers:

Psalm 62

Focus Verse:
[5] Yes, my soul, find rest in God;
my hope comes from him.

Whatever the situation that caused David to write this
Psalm was, it seems that it impacted the whole nation.
Jeduthun was one of the key leaders in the musical
worship in David's kingdom (1 Chronicles 16:42). David
wrote this psalm to encourage the faith of the nation
because he was not just a political or military leader but
also sought to encourage his people to know and honor
God.

For the director of music. For Jeduthun.
A psalm of David.
[1] Truly my soul finds rest in God;
my salvation comes from him.
[2] Truly he is my rock and my salvation;
he is my fortress, I will never be shaken.

[3] How long will you assault me?
Would all of you throw me down—
this leaning wall, this tottering fence?
[4] Surely they intend to topple me
from my lofty place;
they take delight in lies.
With their mouths they bless,
but in their hearts they curse.

[5] Yes, my soul, find rest in God;
my hope comes from him.
[6] Truly he is my rock and my salvation;
he is my fortress, I will not be shaken.

[7] My salvation and my honor depend on God;
   he is my mighty rock, my refuge.
[8] Trust in him at all times, you people;
   pour out your hearts to him,
   for God is our refuge.

[9] Surely the lowborn are but a breath,
   the highborn are but a lie.
If weighed on a balance, they are nothing;
   together they are only a breath.
[10] Do not trust in extortion
   or put vain hope in stolen goods;
though your riches increase,
   do not set your heart on them.

[11] One thing God has spoken,
   two things I have heard:
"Power belongs to you, God,
[12]   and with you, Lord, is unfailing love";
and, "You reward everyone
   according to what they have done."

God is David's rock in whom he finds rest (verses 1-2).
David's enemies have caused him to feel like a tottering
fence (verses 3-4). His central statement of dependence on
God challenges others to trust too (verse 5-8). David
encourages them that because life is so short, they should
not trust in manmade schemes (verses 9-10). Finally,
David concludes with the certain declaration of his
confidence in God's powerful love and justice.

Take a moment to reread the psalm in *The Message*.

[1-2] God, the one and only— I'll wait as long as he says.
  Everything I need comes from him,
    so why not?
  He's solid rock under my feet,
    breathing room for my soul,
  An impregnable castle:
    I'm set for life.

[3-4] How long will you gang up on me?
    How long will you run with the bullies?
  There's nothing to you, any of you—
    rotten floorboards, worm-eaten rafters,
  Anthills plotting to bring down mountains,
    far gone in make-believe.
  You talk a good line,
    but every "blessing" breathes a curse.

[5-6] God, the one and only—
    I'll wait as long as he says.
  Everything I hope for comes from him,
    so why not?
  He's solid rock under my feet,
    breathing room for my soul,
  An impregnable castle:
    I'm set for life.

[7-8] My help and glory are in God
    —granite-strength and safe-harbor-God—
  So trust him absolutely, people;
    lay your lives on the line for him.
    God is a safe place to be.

[9] Man as such is smoke,
    woman as such, a mirage.

Put them together, they're nothing;
  two times nothing is nothing.

[10] And a windfall, if it comes—
  don't make too much of it.

[11] God said this once and for all;
  how many times
 Have I heard it repeated?
  "Strength comes
 Straight from God."

[12] Love to you, Lord God!
  You pay a fair wage for a good day's work!

The focus of this Psalm is the rest that God provides his people when they seem to be under threat of collapse, both individually and as a community. David speaks to the heart of the human question in uncertain times- "Who has the power; and are they loving and just?" David affirms for us that God truly is the one with the power, salvation and stability. What is this salvation? What can we look to this Rock for?

First, David tells us to look to God for rest. This is not necessarily physical rest, but more soul rest. This is connected to physical rest, but deeper. His soul was like a leaning wall, a tottering fence, threatened to be toppled over by assaulting lies. What a leaning and tottering soul needs is a rock and stabilizing structure to keep it from being shaken. How about us? Are our souls at rest? Are we restless in our spirit, unsettled by the lies we hear from the world, our own insecurities and the evil one? David calls us to pour our hearts out to God the Rock, looking to Him for power and truth.

Second, David tells us to look to our Rock for our reputation. David's identity and the reputation of the people of God were threatened. His honor depended on God. When we feel threatened, our reputation or public identity questioned, how do we react? Do we respond trying to control the situation, putting our hope in our vain controlling measures, or do we pour our heart out to God's unfailing love, believing that he rewards all according to what they have done? He is the ultimate judge which we can entrust our reputation.

Prayer:

Father, I need your rest. I look to you as the source of my salvation from my shaking. Give me a firm foundation to plant my life in the midst of the storms around me. I pour out my heart to you, seeking your power to bring me to a place of truth and justice. Amen.

Notes and Personal Prayers:

Psalm 139

Focus Verse:
⁸ If I go up to the heavens, you are there;
if I make my bed in the depths, you are there.

David's intimate conversation with God gives us a glimpse
into the depth of his trust in God's intervention in his life.
He faces rebellious, God-hating, evil-speaking, bloodthirsty and wicked adversaries. It is in times like these
that David is in need of a trusted ally.

For the director of music. Of David. A psalm.
¹ You have searched me, LORD,
and you know me.
² You know when I sit and when I rise;
you perceive my thoughts from afar.
³ You discern my going out and my lying down;
you are familiar with all my ways.
⁴ Before a word is on my tongue
you, LORD, know it completely.
⁵ You hem me in behind and before,
and you lay your hand upon me.
⁶ Such knowledge is too wonderful for me,
too lofty for me to attain.

⁷ Where can I go from your Spirit?
Where can I flee from your presence?
⁸ If I go up to the heavens, you are there;
if I make my bed in the depths, you are there.
⁹ If I rise on the wings of the dawn,
if I settle on the far side of the sea,
¹⁰ even there your hand will guide me,
your right hand will hold me fast.
¹¹ If I say, "Surely the darkness will hide me

and the light become night around me,"
¹² even the darkness will not be dark to you;
   the night will shine like the day,
   for darkness is as light to you.

¹³ For you created my inmost being;
   you knit me together in my mother's womb.
¹⁴ I praise you because I am fearfully and wonderfully made;
   your works are wonderful,
   I know that full well.
¹⁵ My frame was not hidden from you
   when I was made in the secret place,
   when I was woven together in the depths of the earth.
¹⁶ Your eyes saw my unformed body;
   all the days ordained for me were written in your book
   before one of them came to be.
¹⁷ How precious to me are your thoughts, God!
   How vast is the sum of them!
¹⁸ Were I to count them,
   they would outnumber the grains of sand —
   when I awake, I am still with you.

¹⁹ If only you, God, would slay the wicked!
   Away from me, you who are bloodthirsty!
²⁰ They speak of you with evil intent;
   your adversaries misuse your name.
²¹ Do I not hate those who hate you, LORD,
   and abhor those who are in rebellion against you?
²² I have nothing but hatred for them;
   I count them my enemies.
²³ Search me, God, and know my heart;
   test me and know my anxious thoughts.

[24] See if there is any offensive way in me,
  and lead me in the way everlasting.

David acknowledges that God knows his deepest thoughts
and ways (verses 1-6). God's presence will be with him
wherever he goes (verses 7-12). God knows the details of
David's life because He is his Creator (verses 13-18).
David concludes with a prayer for God's intervention
against the wicked and for aid to stay on the everlasting
way (verses 19-24).

David exemplifies vulnerability and transparency before
God. David acknowledges that the details of his life are
not separate from God's providence and care. Often our
hearts and minds are filled with anxiety because we live as
practical atheist (no God) or deist (there is a Source of
creation, but that power has no intervening role in our
daily lives) at best. When our lives are not under the care
of God, we are left to our own ingenuity, which is
accompanied by stress and anxiety.

Take a moment to reread the psalm in *The Message*.

[1-6] GOD, investigate my life; get all the facts firsthand.
  I'm an open book to you;
    even from a distance, you know what I'm thinking.
  You know when I leave and when I get back;
    I'm never out of your sight.
  You know everything I'm going to say
    before I start the first sentence.
  I look behind me and you're there,
    then up ahead and you're there, too—
    your reassuring presence, coming and going.
  This is too much, too wonderful—

I can't take it all in!

7-12 Is there anyplace I can go to avoid your Spirit?
 to be out of your sight?
If I climb to the sky, you're there!
 If I go underground, you're there!
If I flew on morning's wings
 to the far western horizon,
You'd find me in a minute—
 you're already there waiting!
Then I said to myself, "Oh, he even sees me in the dark!
 At night I'm immersed in the light!"
It's a fact: darkness isn't dark to you;
 night and day, darkness and light,
they're all the same to you.

13-16 Oh yes, you shaped me first inside, then out;
 you formed me in my mother's womb.
I thank you, High God—you're breathtaking!
 Body and soul, I am marvelously made!
 I worship in adoration—what a creation!
You know me inside and out,
 you know every bone in my body;
You know exactly how I was made, bit by bit,
 how I was sculpted from nothing into something.
Like an open book, you watched me grow from
conception to birth;
 all the stages of my life were spread out before you,
 The days of my life all prepared
 before I'd even lived one day.

17-22 Your thoughts—how rare, how beautiful!
 God, I'll never comprehend them!
I couldn't even begin to count them—

any more than I could count the sand of the sea.
Oh, let me rise in the morning and live always with you!
    And please, God, do away with wickedness for good!
And you murderers—out of here!—
    all the men and women who belittle you, God,
    infatuated with cheap god-imitations.
See how I hate those who hate you, God,
    see how I loathe all this godless arrogance;
I hate it with pure, unadulterated hatred.
    Your enemies are my enemies!

23-24 Investigate my life, O God,
    find out everything about me;
Cross-examine and test me,
    get a clear picture of what I'm about;
See for yourself whether I've done anything wrong—
    then guide me on the road to eternal life.

David asks God to look deep into his mind and heart in order to see what he wrestles. He asks God to lead him away from self-destructive paths and into a good and eternal way of life. How do we cultivate this type of heart before God?

First, we can entrust our hours, intentions and even words to God's providence. Knowing that from waking to sleeping, he is aware and involved. Second, we are invited to live with an abiding sense that whatever physical location or situation we are in, God is there to guide and hold us fast. Even in the darkest moments, God shines through with perspective, wisdom and his life giving Spirit. Third, we can regularly remind ourselves that our identity is not fundamentally based on who we can make ourselves or what others have conformed us to be. Our primary source of identity is that we have been created with care and purpose by the living God.

When we are laying down in what seems like a desolate and dark place, thoughts filled with anxious fear and in need of a guiding hand down a good path, we can take hope that God's Spirit is with us. He has created and formed us with a purpose. He knows our fears, failures and our future!

Prayer:
Creator and ever-present Lord, I praise you that you are not distant from your people. I ask you to see where I struggle and lack faith. In moments of vulnerability, confusion and weakness, I need your hand to guide me away from evil and into your good and eternal way.
Amen.

Notes and Personal Prayers:

Psalm 141

Focus Verse:
² May my prayer be set before you like incense;
may the lifting up of my hands be like the evening
sacrifice.

David knew throughout his life the struggle to maintain integrity in times of difficulty. While being hunted by Saul, he would not kill Saul and take the throne by his own hand before God's time. Instead, he faithfully waited for God to bring him to the throne as God had promised. When he did experience moral failure, even covering it up for a period, he honestly and humbly received the correction of Nathan the prophet. When David was forced out of his capital by his son Absalom and mocked by bystanders, David walked with integrity, waiting on God's timing to reestablish his throne. In this Psalm, David shows us how to keep perspective in these types of situations.

A psalm of David.
¹ I call to you, LORD, come quickly to me;
   hear me when I call to you.
² May my prayer be set before you like incense;
   may the lifting up of my hands be like the evening
sacrifice.

³ Set a guard over my mouth, LORD;
   keep watch over the door of my lips.
⁴ Do not let my heart be drawn to what is evil
   so that I take part in wicked deeds
along with those who are evildoers;
   do not let me eat their delicacies.

⁵ Let a righteous man strike me—that is a kindness;
    let him rebuke me —that is oil on my head.
My head will not refuse it,
    for my prayer will still be against the deeds of evildoers.
⁶ Their rulers will be thrown down from the cliffs,
    and the wicked will learn
that my words were well spoken.
⁷ They will say, "As one plows and breaks up the earth,
    so our bones have been scattered at the mouth of the
grave."

⁸ But my eyes are fixed on you, Sovereign LORD;
    in you I take refuge —do not give me over to death.
⁹ Keep me safe from the traps set by evildoers,
    from the snares they have laid for me.
¹⁰ Let the wicked fall into their own nets,
    while I pass by in safety.

David begins his evening prayer by asking God to quickly
hear his call (verses 1-2). David prays that in all things he
would walk with integrity (verse 3-4). He asks for help to
respect the righteous and resist the wicked (verse 5-7). He
concludes by fixing his hope on God's protection (verses 8-
10).

David shows us that our evening prayers don't just have
to be about what we fear. David wants God to quickly aid
him. Like a sentry on post, David asks that God would
guard him from both evil inside and outside. He prays
that God would help him avoid evil words, ambitions,
actions and associations.

David also asks God for accountability. He knows that in
every area of life from tactical proficiency to moral purity,

we need accountability. He knows he needs righteous mentors who can guide and even correct him when he goes down the destructive path- men like Nathan, Jonathan and Samuel.

Finally, David gives us a good picture of what to do with the outside threats. Yes, we do need to know them, understand them and avoid them, but if we merely focus on them we will be overwhelmed with fear instead of faith. David, in faith fixes his focus on his Sovereign Lord. Like a warrior focused on the commands of his leader instead of the threats of his enemy, David fixes his eyes on God the High King. He is the one who holds all people and purposes in his ultimate plan and control.

Take a moment to reread the Psalm in *The Message*.

1-2 GOD, come close. Come quickly!
Open your ears—it's my voice you're hearing!
   Treat my prayer as sweet incense rising;
      my raised hands are my evening prayers.

3-7 Post a guard at my mouth, GOD,
      set a watch at the door of my lips.
   Don't let me so much as dream of evil
      or thoughtlessly fall into bad company.
   And these people who only do wrong—
      don't let them lure me with their sweet talk!
   May the Just One set me straight,
      may the Kind One correct me,
   Don't let sin anoint my head.
      I'm praying hard against their evil ways!
   Oh, let their leaders be pushed off a high rock cliff;
      make them face the music.

Like a rock pulverized by a maul,
  let their bones be scattered at the gates of hell.

8-10 But GOD, dear Lord,
  I only have eyes for you.
Since I've run for dear life to you,
  take good care of me.
Protect me from their evil scheming,
  from all their demonic subterfuge.
Let the wicked fall flat on their faces,
  while I walk off without a scratch.

How about us? How can we make our evening prayer a petition with purpose? No matter our circumstances, we can focus on asking God to help us develop our character and integrity. We can ask him for self-control and courageous discipline to cultivate what is good. We can ask him for godly examples and mentors to speak truth and correction to us when needed. We can ask God to help us to have a focused and fixed-faith in him and his purpose, not just the threats of others or our own strengths or weaknesses.

Prayer:

Sovereign Lord, I want my life to be a sweet smelling fragrance to you. I ask you to guard my heart, mouth and actions from evil. Open me up to righteous discipline and correction. Keep my eyes fixed with faith on you. Amen.

Notes and Personal Prayer:

PRAISE IN THE NIGHT

This section of Psalms focuses on David's songs of praise to God in the midst of learning to trust Him through the darkness. Throughout the story of scripture, one of the greatest aids to God's people to get through the struggles of the night is to turn their eyes and voices in praise to God.

When reading these Psalms, you may be able to glean ways and words that you too can express praise to God. Praise is not something we just do as an aside; it is what we were created to do. As humans, we will only function at our best in the context of honoring God with our lives. Praise is also not something based off our feelings, but on the character and reputation of God. It is often in the midst of praising God that our feelings do get clarified and uplifted.

You might begin your time reading each of these Psalms by reading or singing one of the two following hymns:

Come, Thou Almighty King
Words: Anonymous

Come, thou almighty King,
help us thy name to sing,
help us to praise!
Father all glorious,
o'er all victorious,
come and reign over us, Ancient of Days!

Come, thou incarnate Word,
gird on thy mighty sword,
our prayer attend!
Come, and thy people bless,
and give thy word success,
Spirit of holiness, on us descend!

Come, holy Comforter,
thy sacred witness bear
in this glad hour.
Thou who almighty art,
now rule in every heart,
and ne'er from us depart, Spirit of power!

To thee, great One in Three,
eternal praises be,
hence, evermore.
Thy sovereign majesty
may we in glory see,
and to eternity love and adore!

Jesus! What A Friend For Sinners

Words: J. Wilbur Chapman, 1910.

Jesus! what a Friend for sinners!
Jesus! Lover of my soul;
Friends may fail me, foes assail me,
He, my Savior, makes me whole.

Hallelujah! what a Savior!
Hallelujah! what a Friend!
Saving, helping, keeping, loving,
He is with me to the end.

Jesus! what a Strength in weakness!
Let me hide myself in Him.
Tempted, tried, and sometimes failing,
He, my Strength, my victory wins.

Hallelujah! what a Savior!
Hallelujah! what a Friend!
Saving, helping, keeping, loving,
He is with me to the end.

Jesus! what a Guide and Keeper!
While the tempest still is high,
Storms about me, night overtakes me,
He, my Pilot, hears my cry.

Hallelujah! what a Savior!
Hallelujah! what a Friend!
Saving, helping, keeping, loving,
He is with me to the end.

Psalm 8

Focus Verse:

³ When I consider your heavens,
   the work of your fingers,
   the moon and the stars,
   which you have set in place,
⁴ what is mankind that you are mindful of them,
   human beings that you care for them?

For the director of music. According to *gittith*.
A psalm of David.

¹ LORD, our Lord,
   how majestic is your name in all the earth!

You have set your glory
   in the heavens.
² Through the praise of children and infants
   you have established a stronghold against your enemies,
   to silence the foe and the avenger.
³ When I consider your heavens,
   the work of your fingers,
the moon and the stars,
   which you have set in place,
⁴ what is mankind that you are mindful of them,
   human beings that you care for them?

⁵ You have made them a little lower than the angels
   and crowned them with glory and honor.
⁶ You made them rulers over the works of your hands;
   you put everything under their feet:
⁷ all flocks and herds,
   and the animals of the wild,
⁸ the birds in the sky,

and the fish in the sea,
  all that swim the paths of the seas.

⁹ LORD, our Lord,
  how majestic is your name in all the earth!

David begins with praising God's majestic name in verse
1a. He mentions some of the ways that God's majesty is
demonstrated in verses 1b-4. God's majesty is seen
specifically in his empowering of humans to represent him
in creation (verses 5-8). Verse 9 concludes with a
declaration of God's universal splendor.

This Psalm is a short yet profound consideration of God's
greatness. It can help us praise God even in the midst of
the night's uncertainties. It seems probable that David
wrote this Psalm at night, looking at the majesty of God
displayed in the night sky. David invites us to take in the
majesty of God in whatever our situation and inspires us
to rise above in worship

Take a moment to reread the Psalm in *The Message*.

GOD, brilliant Lord,
  yours is a household name.

² Nursing infants gurgle choruses about you;
  toddlers shout the songs
That drown out enemy talk,
  and silence atheist babble.

³⁻⁴ I look up at your macro-skies, dark and enormous,
  your handmade sky-jewelry,
Moon and stars mounted in their settings.

Then I look at my micro-self and wonder,
Why do you bother with us?
    Why take a second look our way?
5-8 Yet we've so narrowly missed being gods,
    bright with Eden's dawn light.
You put us in charge of your handcrafted world,
    repeated to us your Genesis-charge,
Made us lords of sheep and cattle,
    even animals out in the wild,
Birds flying and fish swimming,
    whales singing in the ocean deeps.

9 GOD, brilliant Lord,
    your name echoes around the world.

Our praise in the night is rooted in God's personal
character. David tells us that God's name is majestic over
all the earth. He means that the greatness of God's
character, reputation and identity are made known
throughout all of his creation. His character is majestic-
amazing, profound, awe-inspiring, and awesome. Take
time to consider the different ways God has revealed
himself around you and in creation.

David also tells us that we can see God's greatness by how
he uses the weak to overcome the strong. God's power is
revealed in faithful honor and trust in him even in the
midst of human weakness (like a child). This power is
greater than any prideful human strength of those who
mock God and his people. As you look at your life, when
have you seen God work powerfully in the midst of your
weakness? Trust in a mighty God is a sign of true
strength!

The final thing that David praises God for is how God has entrusted to humans the responsibility of honorable care and stewardship of the creation. God has created you with purpose and responsibility. Moments of darkness might come upon us when we are confused about what our purpose really is or where we are supposed to invest our lives. David invites us to stop and praise God for entrusting us with representing him in our world. While you may face times of despair, look toward God with a worshipping heart and draw near to him. He will be your source of direction, guiding you in how to live out your God-given purposes and potential.

Prayer:

Majestic Creator, you have made the great wonders of creation. You have made you power shown through the weakness of men. I consider your ways and works and worship you. In the midst of moments of darkness, turn my eyes in praise to you. Amen.

Notes and Personal Prayer:

Psalm 18

Focus Verse:
[28] You, LORD, keep my lamp burning;
my God turns my darkness into light.

David often experienced great deliverances from God over his enemies. This Psalm praises God for coming to David's aid in the midst of battle. The introductory notes may indicate that David wrote this Psalm to celebrate God's deliverance from many different battles and from the violent jealousy of Saul.

For the director of music. Of David the servant of the LORD. He sang to the LORD the words of this song when the LORD delivered him from the hand of all his enemies and from the hand of Saul. He said:
[1] I love you, LORD, my strength.

[2] The LORD is my rock, my fortress and my deliverer;
my God is my rock, in whom I take refuge,
my shield and the horn of my salvation, my stronghold.

[3] I called to the LORD, who is worthy of praise,
and I have been saved from my enemies.
[4] The cords of death entangled me;
the torrents of destruction overwhelmed me.
[5] The cords of the grave coiled around me;
the snares of death confronted me.

[6] In my distress I called to the LORD;
I cried to my God for help.
From his temple he heard my voice;
my cry came before him, into his ears.
[7] The earth trembled and quaked,

and the foundations of the mountains shook;
　　they trembled because he was angry.
⁸ Smoke rose from his nostrils;
　　consuming fire came from his mouth,
　　burning coals blazed out of it.
⁹ He parted the heavens and came down;
　　dark clouds were under his feet.
¹⁰ He mounted the cherubim and flew;
　　he soared on the wings of the wind.
¹¹ He made darkness his covering, his canopy around
him—
　　the dark rain clouds of the sky.
¹² Out of the brightness of his presence clouds advanced,
　　with hailstones and bolts of lightning.
¹³ The LORD thundered from heaven;
　　the voice of the Most High resounded.
¹⁴ He shot his arrows and scattered the enemy,
　　with great bolts of lightning he routed them.
¹⁵ The valleys of the sea were exposed
　　and the foundations of the earth laid bare
at your rebuke, LORD,
　　at the blast of breath from your nostrils.

¹⁶ He reached down from on high and took hold of me;
　　he drew me out of deep waters.
¹⁷ He rescued me from my powerful enemy,
　　from my foes, who were too strong for me.
¹⁸ They confronted me in the day of my disaster,
　　but the LORD was my support.
¹⁹ He brought me out into a spacious place;
　　he rescued me because he delighted in me.

²⁰ The LORD has dealt with me according to my
righteousness;

according to the cleanness of my hands he has rewarded me.

21 For I have kept the ways of the LORD;
    I am not guilty of turning from my God.

22 All his laws are before me;
    I have not turned away from his decrees.

23 I have been blameless before him
    and have kept myself from sin.

24 The LORD has rewarded me according to my righteousness,
    according to the cleanness of my hands in his sight.

25 To the faithful you show yourself faithful,
    to the blameless you show yourself blameless,

26 to the pure you show yourself pure,
    but to the devious you show yourself shrewd.

27 You save the humble
    but bring low those whose eyes are haughty.

28 You, LORD, keep my lamp burning;
    my God turns my darkness into light.

29 With your help I can advance against a troop;
    with my God I can scale a wall.

30 As for God, his way is perfect:
    The LORD's word is flawless;
    he shields all who take refuge in him.

31 For who is God besides the LORD?
    And who is the Rock except our God?

32 It is God who arms me with strength
    and keeps my way secure.

33 He makes my feet like the feet of a deer;
    he causes me to stand on the heights.

34 He trains my hands for battle;
    my arms can bend a bow of bronze.

³⁵ You make your saving help my shield,
and your right hand sustains me;
your help has made me great.
³⁶ You provide a broad path for my feet,
so that my ankles do not give way.

³⁷ I pursued my enemies and overtook them;
I did not turn back till they were destroyed.
³⁸ I crushed them so that they could not rise;
they fell beneath my feet.
³⁹ You armed me with strength for battle;
you humbled my adversaries before me.
⁴⁰ You made my enemies turn their backs in flight,
and I destroyed my foes.
⁴¹ They cried for help, but there was no one to save them
to the LORD, but he did not answer.
⁴² I beat them as fine as windblown dust;
I trampled them like mud in the streets.
⁴³ You have delivered me from the attacks of the people;
you have made me the head of nations.
People I did not know now serve me,
⁴⁴   foreigners cower before me;
as soon as they hear of me, they obey me.
⁴⁵ They all lose heart;
they come trembling from their strongholds.

⁴⁶ The LORD lives! Praise be to my Rock!
Exalted be God my Savior!
⁴⁷ He is the God who avenges me,
who subdues nations under me,
⁴⁸   who saves me from my enemies.
You exalted me above my foes;
from a violent man you rescued me.

⁴⁹ Therefore I will praise you, LORD, among the nations;
   I will sing the praises of your name.

⁵⁰ He gives his king great victories;
   he shows unfailing love to his anointed,
   to David and to his descendants forever.

David begins by summarizing God's faithful character
(verses 1-2). He specifically recounts how God rescued
him out of the brink of death (verses 3-5). David describes
God's aid like a great ragging thunderstorm pounding his
enemies (verses 6-15). God moved David from a place of
threat to spacious security (verses 16-19). God's acts on
behalf of David were tied to David's loyalty to Him
(verses 20-24). David encourages all to have a loyal
relationship with God (verses 25-29). Again, David gets
specific about God's deliverance and aid in the midst of
battle (verses 30-36), and how God gave him victory over
his enemies (verses 37-45 and 46-49). Finally, David
reaffirms God's loyalty to his chosen and faithful one
(verse 50).

Take a moment to reread the Psalm in *The Message*.

¹⁻² I love you, GOD— you make me strong.
   GOD is bedrock under my feet,
      the castle in which I live,
      my rescuing knight.
   My God—the high crag
      where I run for dear life,
      hiding behind the boulders,
      safe in the granite hideout.

³ I sing to GOD, the Praise-Lofty,

and find myself safe and saved.

4-5 The hangman's noose was tight at my throat;
   devil waters rushed over me.
 Hell's ropes cinched me tight;
   death traps barred every exit.

6 A hostile world! I call to GOD,
   I cry to God to help me.
 From his palace he hears my call;
   my cry brings me right into his presence—
   a private audience!

7-15 Earth wobbles and lurches;
   huge mountains shake like leaves,
 Quake like aspen leaves
   because of his rage.
 His nostrils flare, bellowing smoke;
   his mouth spits fire.
 Tongues of fire dart in and out;
   he lowers the sky.
 He steps down;
   under his feet an abyss opens up.
 He's riding a winged creature,
   swift on wind-wings.
 Now he's wrapped himself
   in a trenchcoat of black-cloud darkness.
 But his cloud-brightness bursts through,
   spraying hailstones and fireballs.
 Then GOD thundered out of heaven;
   the High God gave a great shout,
   spraying hailstones and fireballs.
 God shoots his arrows—pandemonium!
   He hurls his lightnings—a rout!

The secret sources of ocean are exposed,
   the hidden depths of earth lie uncovered
The moment you roar in protest,
   let loose your hurricane anger.

16-19 But me he caught—reached all the way
   from sky to sea; he pulled me out
Of that ocean of hate, that enemy chaos,
   the void in which I was drowning.
They hit me when I was down,
   but GOD stuck by me.
He stood me up on a wide-open field;
   I stood there saved—surprised to be loved!

20-24 GOD made my life complete
   when I placed all the pieces before him.
When I got my act together,
   he gave me a fresh start.
Now I'm alert to GOD's ways;
   I don't take God for granted.
Every day I review the ways he works;
   I try not to miss a trick.
I feel put back together,
   and I'm watching my step.
GOD rewrote the text of my life
   when I opened the book of my heart to his eyes.

25-27 The good people taste your goodness,
The whole people taste your health,
The true people taste your truth,
The bad ones can't figure you out.
You take the side of the down-and-out,
But the stuck-up you take down a peg.

$^{28-29}$ Suddenly, GOD, you floodlight my life;
    I'm blazing with glory, God's glory!
I smash the bands of marauders,
    I vault the highest fences.

^{30} What a God! His road
    stretches straight and smooth.
Every GOD-direction is road-tested.
    Everyone who runs toward him
Makes it.

$^{31-42}$ Is there any god like GOD?
    Are we not at bedrock?
Is not this the God who armed me,
    then aimed me in the right direction?
Now I run like a deer;
    I'm king of the mountain.
He shows me how to fight;
    I can bend a bronze bow!
You protect me with salvation-armor;
    you hold me up with a firm hand,
    caress me with your gentle ways.
You cleared the ground under me
    so my footing was firm.
When I chased my enemies I caught them;
    I didn't let go till they were dead men.
I nailed them; they were down for good;
    then I walked all over them.
You armed me well for this fight,
    you smashed the upstarts.
You made my enemies turn tail,
    and I wiped out the haters.
They cried "uncle"
    but Uncle didn't come;

They yelled for GOD
  and got no for an answer.
I ground them to dust; they gusted in the wind.
  I threw them out, like garbage in the gutter.

43-45 You rescued me from a squabbling people;
  you made me a leader of nations.
People I'd never heard of served me;
  the moment they got wind of me they listened.
The foreign devils gave up; they came
  on their bellies, crawling from their hideouts.

46-48 Live, GOD! Blessings from my Rock,
  my free and freeing God, towering!
This God set things right for me
  and shut up the people who talked back.
He rescued me from enemy anger,
  he pulled me from the grip of upstarts,
He saved me from the bullies.

49-50 That's why I'm thanking you, GOD,
  all over the world.
That's why I'm singing songs
  that rhyme your name.
God's king takes the trophy;
  God's chosen is beloved.
I mean David and all his children—
  always.

Many children fear the dark. There is something about
darkness that is full of mystery and potential danger.
Before the days of night-vision goggles, warriors knew the
danger that darkness brought. Even with our great

technologies, darkness is still a time in which our enemy can take advantage of us.

When we face certain unknown threats it may seem like we are in the dark and vulnerable. This can be with a physical enemy or it could be with a family relationship or professional uncertainty. We will find it hard to rest, when we are vulnerable and in the dark. We may stay on edge and unable to entrust ourselves to the available resources.

David challenges us to listen to his story of God's faithfulness. God's ability to deal with David's darkness was not based on him keeping the watch fire going all night. It was the LORD who kept his lamp burning as he stood watch over His servant David.

What areas of darkness, uncertainty, and vulnerability do you face that keep you from rest? Write them down in a journal or something similar. Entrust them to the Lord's watch. Ask him to bring the brightness of his presence into those areas. Allow him to arm you with strength to face the battle ahead.

Prayer:
God my Rock and Shield, you know the things that threaten to entangle me. I ask for your powerful presence to come close. Help me to walk faithfully in your flawless word. I entrust these battles into your sustaining strength.
Amen.

Notes and Personal Prayer:

Psalm 30

Focus Verse:

[5] For his anger lasts only a moment,
but his favor lasts a lifetime;
weeping may stay for the night,
but rejoicing comes in the morning.

David wrote this Psalm looking to the future when the nation would dedicate the new temple after his death. He wanted them as individuals and as the people of God to know that there will be times when it is as if they are deep in a pit of sorrow from their own sin or the sins of others. There will be times of weeping, wailing and repentance. Yet, God will hear the cry of the broken hearted when they ask for help. He will move them into a new day of rejoicing- out of darkness and into dancing with songs of joy and praise. Much of the story of David's life as recounted in this Psalm would serve as a model for the nation in their worship and devotion to God.

A psalm. A song. For the dedication of the temple. Of David.

[1] I will exalt you, LORD,
for you lifted me out of the depths
and did not let my enemies gloat over me.
[2] LORD my God, I called to you for help,
and you healed me.
[3] You, LORD, brought me up from the realm of the dead;
you spared me from going down to the pit.

[4] Sing the praises of the LORD, you his faithful people;
praise his holy name.
[5] For his anger lasts only a moment,
but his favor lasts a lifetime;

weeping may stay for the night,
  but rejoicing comes in the morning.

6 When I felt secure, I said,
  "I will never be shaken."
7 LORD, when you favored me,
  you made my royal mountain stand firm;
but when you hid your face,
  I was dismayed.

8 To you, LORD, I called;
  to the Lord I cried for mercy:
9 "What is gained if I am silenced,
  if I go down to the pit?
Will the dust praise you?
  Will it proclaim your faithfulness?
10 Hear, LORD, and be merciful to me;
  LORD, be my help. "

11 You turned my wailing into dancing;
  you removed my sackcloth and clothed me with joy,
12 that my heart may sing your praises and not be silent.
  LORD my God, I will praise you forever.

David begins this Psalm by recounting God's help and
healing in his life (verses 1-3). He praises God that His
mercy does not leave us in the misery of our sin when we
call to him (verses 4-5). David remembers the security
found in God's favor (verses 6-7) and asks for God's mercy
to not abandon him in death (verses 8-10). David
concludes by praising God for bringing him through
sorrow to songs of joy (verses 11-12).

Take a moment to reread the Psalm in *The Message*.

¹ I give you all the credit, GOD—
you got me out of that mess,
    you didn't let my foes gloat.

²⁻³ GOD, my God, I yelled for help
    and you put me together.
  GOD, you pulled me out of the grave,
    gave me another chance at life
    when I was down-and-out.

⁴⁻⁵ All you saints! Sing your hearts out to GOD!
    Thank him to his face!
  He gets angry once in a while, but across
    a lifetime there is only love.
  The nights of crying your eyes out
    give way to days of laughter.

⁶⁻⁷ When things were going great
    I crowed, "I've got it made.
  I'm GOD's favorite.
    He made me king of the mountain."
  Then you looked the other way
    and I fell to pieces.

⁸⁻¹⁰ I called out to you, GOD;
    I laid my case before you:
  "Can you sell me for a profit when I'm dead?
    auction me off at a cemetery yard sale?
  When I'm 'dust to dust' my songs
    and stories of you won't sell.
  So listen! and be kind!
    Help me out of this!"

[11-12] You did it: you changed wild lament
      into whirling dance;
  You ripped off my black mourning band
      and decked me with wildflowers.
  I'm about to burst with song;
      I can't keep quiet about you.
  GOD, my God,
      I can't thank you enough.

David shows us a pattern of worship for the people of God. The temple was a place of praise for the nation, and this Psalm is written just for that. He shows us that our praise should include our story. What type of situation where we in? David uses words like depths, gloated over, realm of the dead and pit. What words would you use to describe your situation? David tells us what God did- lifted up, healed, brought up, spared, turned wailing into dancing. What words would you use to describe God's actions on your behalf?

David also says that praise in the night is better when it is done in God's presence with God's people. He calls for the faithful people of God to sing the praises of God together. Do you have a place where you can gather in God's presence with God's people to sing and praise God for his acts? What would this look like? David uses words like- exalt, sing, and dance. Think about how your story could inspire others to praise and honor God.

Prayer:
Yahweh, I praise you and exalt you for lifting me up out of the depths. Help me to call others to worship and experience your presence and care. Turn my wailing into dancing and mourning into joyful songs of praise. Amen.

Notes and Personal Prayers:

Psalm 63

Focus Verses:
[6] On my bed I remember you;
I think of you through the watches of the night.

David writes this Psalm in a physically and politically difficult location (the dry desert of Judah and the revolt of his son Absalom- 2 Samuel 15-19). Yet, he does not allow those uncertainties to paralyze him with anxiety and fear.

A psalm of David. When he was in the Desert of Judah.

[1] You, God, are my God,
    earnestly I seek you;
I thirst for you,
    my whole being longs for you,
in a dry and parched land
    where there is no water.

[2] I have seen you in the sanctuary
    and beheld your power and your glory.
[3] Because your love is better than life,
    my lips will glorify you.
[4] I will praise you as long as I live,
    and in your name I will lift up my hands.
[5] I will be fully satisfied as with the richest of foods;
    with singing lips my mouth will praise you.

[6] On my bed I remember you;
    I think of you through the watches of the night.
[7] Because you are my help,
    I sing in the shadow of your wings.
[8] I cling to you;
    your right hand upholds me.

⁹ Those who want to kill me will be destroyed;
  they will go down to the depths of the earth.
¹⁰ They will be given over to the sword
  and become food for jackals.

¹¹ But the king will rejoice in God;
  all who swear by God will glory in him,
  while the mouths of liars will be silenced.

In a barren place, David expresses his deep thirst for God
(verse 1). David's greatest delight is to worship God
(verses 2-5). Even into the night hours, David fixes his
thoughts on God (verses 6-8). His hope is in God's justice
to be brought to his enemies (verses 9-10). David
concludes by reinforcing his commitment to rejoice in
God's providence and care (verse 11).

Take a moment to reread the psalm in *The Message.*

¹ God—you're my God! I can't get enough of you!
  I've worked up such hunger and thirst for God,
    traveling across dry and weary deserts.

²⁻⁴ So here I am in the place of worship, eyes open,
    drinking in your strength and glory.
  In your generous love I am really living at last!
    My lips brim praises like fountains.
  I bless you every time I take a breath;
    My arms wave like banners of praise to you.

⁵⁻⁸ I eat my fill of prime rib and gravy;
    I smack my lips. It's time to shout praises!
  If I'm sleepless at midnight,
    I spend the hours in grateful reflection.

Because you've always stood up for me,
   I'm free to run and play.
I hold on to you for dear life,
   and you hold me steady as a post.

9-11 Those who are out to get me are marked for doom,
   marked for death, bound for hell.
They'll die violent deaths;
   jackals will tear them limb from limb.
But the king is glad in God;
   his true friends spread the joy,
While small-minded gossips
   are gagged for good.

When we face situations like David, our beds may not be a
place of peace. Instead, our thoughts may be flooded with
fear, worry and confusion. David shows us that we can
come to these situations with a greater sense of hope and
joy. Just as stress and fear can impact our whole body, so
can our worship. He says that his whole being longs for
God. He says that with his lips he will sing and glorify,
and with his hands he will lift up praise. He even says
that just as his appetite is satisfied with good foods, he will
find satisfaction with God- not just the things God will
give him. There is great benefit from involving our bodies
in worship.

David shows us that when we have a single-hearted
devotion and delight in God, the threats to our security,
our reputation, our internal conflict or opinions of others
do not impact us as deeply because our focus is on him.
This is why David could say that God's love is better than
life!

What physical acts do you involve yourself in to express your relationship with God? Like any relationship, there will be some form of physical involvement. It could be speaking out loud the things you are thankful to God. It could be raising your hands in private or public in prayer or song as a sign of praise and honor. It could be kneeling in prayerful humility and dependence or standing as a sign of respect and readiness to listen and obey. It could mean physically fasting as a sign of not living by bread alone but by every word of God.

As we allow our relationship with God to have deeper and more robust expression (not just ritual exercises), we will see how our thoughts and affections focus more on him and less on the growing anxiety of the day or night.

Prayer:
Satisfying God, I desire a relationship with you that is alive and refreshing. I rejoice in you. I thirst for your presence in the midst of my life. Help me to seek you more and more with my whole self. Amen.

Notes and Personal Prayers:

Psalm 65

[8] The whole earth is filled with awe at your wonders;
    where morning dawns, where evening fades,
        you call forth songs of joy.

Throughout David's reign, he was passionate about God's presence being with his people. David proclaims that in his city, on the mountain of God they are standing ready with praise for God. One of the great stories of David's reign is when after much work, he is able to bring the Ark of the Covenant to a tabernacle in Jerusalem (1 Chronicles 15-16). Later, he focused on preparations for a new temple to be built by his son Solomon.

For the director of music. A psalm of David. A song.

[1] Praise awaits you, our God, in Zion;
    to you our vows will be fulfilled.
[2] You who answer prayer,
    to you all people will come.
[3] When we were overwhelmed by sins,
    you forgave our transgressions.
[4] Blessed are those you choose
    and bring near to live in your courts!
We are filled with the good things of your house,
    of your holy temple.

[5] You answer us with awesome and righteous deeds,
    God our Savior,
the hope of all the ends of the earth
    and of the farthest seas,
[6] who formed the mountains by your power,
    having armed yourself with strength,
[7] who stilled the roaring of the seas,

the roaring of their waves,
and the turmoil of the nations.
⁸ The whole earth is filled with awe at your wonders;
where morning dawns, where evening fades,
you call forth songs of joy.

⁹ You care for the land and water it;
you enrich it abundantly.
The streams of God are filled with water
to provide the people with grain,
for so you have ordained it.
¹⁰ You drench its furrows and level its ridges;
you soften it with showers and bless its crops.
¹¹ You crown the year with your bounty,
and your carts overflow with abundance.
¹² The grasslands of the wilderness overflow;
the hills are clothed with gladness.
¹³ The meadows are covered with flocks
and the valleys are mantled with grain;
they shout for joy and sing.

David praises God for bringing his people into His presence (verses 1-4). He recounts how God has preformed awesome deeds in response to His people's cries (verses 5-8). David concludes by reflecting on God's faithful care for all of creation (verses 9-13).

Take a moment to reread the Psalm in *The Message*.

¹⁻² Silence is praise to you, Zion-dwelling God,
And also obedience.
You hear the prayer in it all.

²⁻⁸ We all arrive at your doorstep sooner

or later, loaded with guilt,
Our sins too much for us—
   but you get rid of them once and for all.
Blessed are the chosen! Blessed the guest
   at home in your place!
We expect our fill of good things
   in your house, your heavenly manse.
All your salvation wonders
   are on display in your trophy room.
Earth-Tamer, Ocean-Pourer,
   Mountain-Maker, Hill-Dresser,
Muzzler of sea storm and wave crash,
   of mobs in noisy riot—
Far and wide they'll come to a stop,
   they'll stare in awe, in wonder.
Dawn and dusk take turns
   calling, "Come and worship."

9-13 Oh, visit the earth,
   ask her to join the dance!
Deck her out in spring showers,
   fill the God-River with living water.
Paint the wheat fields golden.
   Creation was made for this!
Drench the plowed fields,
   soak the dirt clods
With rainfall as harrow and rake
   bring her to blossom and fruit.
Snow-crown the peaks with splendor,
   scatter rose petals down your paths,
All through the wild meadows, rose petals.
   Set the hills to dancing,
Dress the canyon walls with live sheep,
   a drape of flax across the valleys.

Let them shout, and shout, and shout!
Oh, oh, let them sing!

Sometimes the hardest part of getting through our seasons of darkness is believing that God will hear and answer. David tells us that with each new morning, God calls forth songs of praise by His awesome works. What are some of these mighty acts that inspire choruses of worship?

First, God answers the prayers of those who come to him. He forgives them when they are overwhelmed with sin. He brings them back into his good and blessed presence. Second, God stands as the creator and sustainer of all creation, even its greatest wonders and powers. When we face a night of uncertainty, David reminds us that the morning will remind us who truly has made, sustains and blesses us. The difficulties of the upcoming morning need not overwhelm us with fear or frustration. We can sing songs of faith-filled joy, knowing that God has initiated reconciliation with us. He calls us to receive his forgiveness and enter into his presence each morning.

As we examine our lives, what might be the sins that overwhelm us and keep us from God's presence? Confess them to God and lean into God's mercy. What are the areas of our lives that need order and forming? Ask God for the wisdom and strength to bring His good purpose and priorities into your life. What thoughts or situations seem to be roaring uncontrolled and full of turmoil? Seek for God's stillness and peace. Ask Him to take away your anxiety and replace it with awe at His great works. What are the relationships that need care, healing, life, and refreshing? Ask God to bring his cleansing, enriching and joy giving provision into the midst of them.

Prayer:

God our Savior, the greatest thing for me to know is your joy-filling presence. May I find my greatest delight there. I seek your life giving, forming and filling in my life. May my heart be filled with songs of joy each morning at your awesome deeds. Amen.

Notes and Personal Prayers:

HOPE FOR THE MORNING

This section of Psalms focuses on David's example of looking with hope to the morning. David shows us in various ways that while people my face times of darkness, discouragement and distress, we can trust that God is always at work and will bring us to a new morning on the other side of the darkness. Throughout the Scriptures, God illustrated his promise of future hope by the rising of the sun and the lack of night. The Hebrew Prophet Malachi prophesied the future day when God would bring ultimate justice and restoration:

But for you who revere my name, the sun of righteousness will rise with healing in its rays (Malachi 4:2).

Ultimately, the Apostle John prophesied when God would reside with his people forever:

Then the angel showed me the river of the water of life, as clear as crystal, flowing from the throne of God and of the Lamb ² down the middle of the great street of the city. On each side of the river stood the tree of life, bearing twelve crops of fruit, yielding its fruit every month. And the leaves of the tree are for the healing of the nations. ³ No longer will there be any curse. The throne of God and of the Lamb will be in the city, and his servants will serve him. ⁴ They will see his face, and his name will be on their foreheads. ⁵ There will be no more night. They will not need the light of a lamp or the light of the sun, for the Lord God will give them light. And they will reign for ever and ever (Revelation 22:1-5).

When reading these Psalms, you have the opportunity to cultivate hope in God for your life and all of history. Like David, this hope is not based on your own ability to control a situation but on God's perfect purpose and power. These Psalms invite you to place not just your concerns but all of yourself in God's good hands.

You might begin your time reading each of these Psalms by reading or singing one of the two following hymns:

Be Still My Soul
Words: Katharina A. von Schlegel, 1752

Be still, my soul: the Lord is on thy side.
Bear patiently the cross of grief or pain.
Leave to thy God to order and provide;
In every change, He faithful will remain.
Be still, my soul: thy best, thy heavenly Friend
Through thorny ways leads to a joyful end.

Be still, my soul: thy God doth undertake
To guide the future, as He has the past.
Thy hope, thy confidence let nothing shake;
All now mysterious shall be bright at last.
Be still, my soul: the waves and winds still know
His voice Who ruled them while He dwelt below.

Be still, my soul: the hour is hastening on
When we shall be forever with the Lord.
When disappointment, grief and fear are gone,
Sorrow forgot, love's purest joys restored.
Be still, my soul: when change and tears are past
All safe and blessèd we shall meet at last.

Be still, my soul: begin the song of praise
On earth, believing, to Thy Lord on high;
Acknowledge Him in all thy words and ways,
So shall He view thee with a well pleased eye.
Be still, my soul: the Sun of life divine
Through passing clouds shall but more brightly shine.

Like a River Glorious
Words: Frances R. Havergal, 1876

Like a river glorious, is God's perfect peace,
Over all victorious, in its bright increase;
Perfect, yet it floweth, fuller every day,
Perfect, yet it groweth, deeper all the way.

Stayed upon Jehovah, hearts are fully blest
Finding, as He promised, perfect peace and rest.

Hidden in the hollow of His blessed hand,
Never foe can follow, never traitor stand;
Not a surge of worry, not a shade of care,
Not a blast of hurry touch the spirit there.

Stayed upon Jehovah, hearts are fully blest
Finding, as He promised, perfect peace and rest.

Every joy or trial falleth from above,
Traced upon our dial by the Sun of Love;
We may trust Him fully all for us to do.
They who trust Him wholly find Him wholly true.

Stayed upon Jehovah, hearts are fully blest
Finding, as He promised, perfect peace and rest.

Psalm 5

Focus Verse:

³ In the morning, LORD, you hear my voice;
in the morning I lay my requests before you
and wait expectantly.

This morning psalm of David looks to God with eager expectation for Him to lead him through a time when David has been onslaught with the lies and malice of his enemies.

For the director of music. For pipes.
A psalm of David.

¹ Listen to my words, LORD,
consider my lament.
² Hear my cry for help,
my King and my God,
for to you I pray.

³ In the morning, LORD, you hear my voice;
in the morning I lay my requests before you
and wait expectantly.
⁴ For you are not a God who is pleased with wickedness;
with you, evil people are not welcome.
⁵ The arrogant cannot stand
in your presence.
You hate all who do wrong;
⁶ you destroy those who tell lies.
The bloodthirsty and deceitful
you, LORD, detest.
⁷ But I, by your great love,
can come into your house;
in reverence I bow down
toward your holy temple.

^{8} Lead me, LORD, in your righteousness
because of my enemies—
make your way straight before me.
^{9} Not a word from their mouth can be trusted;
their heart is filled with malice.
Their throat is an open grave;
with their tongues they tell lies.
^{10} Declare them guilty, O God!
Let their intrigues be their downfall.
Banish them for their many sins,
for they have rebelled against you.
^{11} But let all who take refuge in you be glad;
let them ever sing for joy.
Spread your protection over them,
that those who love your name may rejoice in you.

^{12} Surely, LORD, you bless the righteous;
you surround them with your favor as with a shield.

David cries out to God for him to listen and hear his
lament (verses 1-2). In verses 3-7, David contrasts God's
love for the humble and hate for the prideful. David more
fully describes his enemies threatening words and asks
God to be his guide and refuge through them (verses 8-
11). Finally, David declares his confidence in God to
shield the righteous (verse 12).

David shows us how he puts hope into action. He puts
himself in the God honoring path- loving and waiting
humility. David refused to align himself with a life that
mimics his enemies who are full of false, deadly, and
rebellious threats. Instead, he petitions God to guide him
down his straight and right path.

Take a moment to reread the Psalm in *The Message*.

1-3 Listen, GOD! Please, pay attention!
Can you make sense of these ramblings,
my groans and cries?
King-God, I need your help.
    Every morning
        you'll hear me at it again.
    Every morning
        I lay out the pieces of my life
        on your altar
        and watch for fire to descend.

4-6 You don't socialize with Wicked,
        or invite Evil over as your houseguest.
    Hot-Air-Boaster collapses in front of you;
        you shake your head over Mischief-Maker.
    God destroys Lie-Speaker;
        Blood-Thirsty and Truth-Bender disgust you.

7-8 And here I am, your invited guest—
        it's incredible!
    I enter your house; here I am,
        prostrate in your inner sanctum,
    Waiting for directions
        to get me safely through enemy lines.

9-10 Every word they speak is a land mine;
        their lungs breathe out poison gas.
    Their throats are gaping graves,
        their tongues slick as mudslides.
    Pile on the guilt, God!
        Let their so-called wisdom wreck them.

Kick them out! They've had their chance.

11-12 But you'll welcome us with open arms
    when we run for cover to you.
  Let the party last all night!
    Stand guard over our celebration.
  You are famous, God, for welcoming God-seekers,
    for decking us out in delight.

How does David model for us hope for each new
morning? First, he invites us into a personal relationship
with God. He says, "My King and my God." David
knows that hope and faith can only happen in the context
of an authentic relationship of trust. For David, this
relationship is cultivated each new morning as he enters
reverently into God's presence- not because of his own
greatness, but because of God's gracious invitation. He
knows that here, God hears his voice as he lays out his
requests. Because of this relationship, David can wait
expectantly for God to lead him in the best way.

As we seek to foster hope for the new day, we must ask
ourselves about our relationship with God? Do we only
know him distantly, or can we confidently say- he is "my
King and my God?" He is the one that has active
authority and care in our lives. Everybody has a
relationship with God, for some it is antagonistic or
apathetic, but others it is anticipating. As you anticipate
reconnecting with a loved one after a long journey, your
relationship with God can be filled with anticipation based
off of a deepening relationship with him.

As we lay our request before him to take and fashion
according to his purpose, we can also ask him to lead us

through the traps and dangers that await us. Hope is not based off an absence of fear or danger. It is a certainty that God will surround us as a shield through the threat, according to his purpose for us in it. Each evening or morning we have the opportunity to ask God specifically to lead us through the situations that we face ahead. It could be an upcoming combat mission, relationship difficulty, leadership responsibility or personal area of development. For some, writing these down in a prayer journal may help.

Prayer:

My King and My God, you are a shield to your people. Your house is a place of hope and love. You know the deadly and deceptive threats that your people face. Help me to navigate through these. Give me a regular time each day to cultivate a relationship of hope and anticipation in you. Amen.

Notes and Personal Prayers:

Psalm 37

[6] He will make your righteous reward
shine like the dawn,
your vindication like the noonday sun.

This psalm shows us David's wisdom when struggling
with injustice and the evil around him. He gives us
insight in how to maintain the right focus and understand
the larger picture.

Of David.

[1] Do not fret because of those who are evil
   or be envious of those who do wrong;
[2] for like the grass they will soon wither,
   like green plants they will soon die away.

[3] Trust in the LORD and do good;
   dwell in the land and enjoy safe pasture.
[4] Take delight in the LORD,
   and he will give you the desires of your heart.

[5] Commit your way to the LORD;
   trust in him and he will do this:
[6] He will make your righteous reward shine like the dawn,
   your vindication like the noonday sun.

[7] Be still before the LORD
   and wait patiently for him;
do not fret when people succeed in their ways,
   when they carry out their wicked schemes.

[8] Refrain from anger and turn from wrath;
   do not fret—it leads only to evil.

⁹ For those who are evil will be destroyed,
    but those who hope in the LORD will inherit the land.

¹⁰ A little while, and the wicked will be no more;
    though you look for them, they will not be found.
¹¹ But the meek will inherit the land
    and enjoy peace and prosperity.

¹² The wicked plot against the righteous
    and gnash their teeth at them;
¹³ but the Lord laughs at the wicked,
    for he knows their day is coming.

¹⁴ The wicked draw the sword
    and bend the bow
to bring down the poor and needy,
    to slay those whose ways are upright.
¹⁵ But their swords will pierce their own hearts,
    and their bows will be broken.

¹⁶ Better the little that the righteous have
    than the wealth of many wicked;
¹⁷ for the power of the wicked will be broken,
    but the LORD upholds the righteous.

¹⁸ The blameless spend their days under the LORD's
care,   and their inheritance will endure forever.
¹⁹ In times of disaster they will not wither;
    in days of famine they will enjoy plenty.

²⁰ But the wicked will perish:
    Though the LORD's enemies are like the flowers of the
field,   they will be consumed, they will go up in smoke.

²¹ The wicked borrow and do not repay,
    but the righteous give generously;
²² those the L<small>ORD</small> blesses will inherit the land,
    but those he curses will be destroyed.

²³ The L<small>ORD</small> makes firm the steps
    of the one who delights in him;
²⁴ though he may stumble, he will not fall,
    for the L<small>ORD</small> upholds him with his hand.

²⁵ I was young and now I am old,
    yet I have never seen the righteous forsaken
    or their children begging bread.
²⁶ They are always generous and lend freely;
    their children will be a blessing.

²⁷ Turn from evil and do good;
    then you will dwell in the land forever.
²⁸ For the L<small>ORD</small> loves the just
    and will not forsake his faithful ones.

Wrongdoers will be completely destroyed;
    the offspring of the wicked will perish.
²⁹ The righteous will inherit the land
    and dwell in it forever.
³⁰ The mouths of the righteous utter wisdom,
    and their tongues speak what is just.
³¹ The law of their God is in their hearts;
    their feet do not slip.

³² The wicked lie in wait for the righteous,
    intent on putting them to death;
³³ but the L<small>ORD</small> will not leave them

in the power of the wicked
  or let them be condemned when brought to trial.

[34] Hope in the LORD
  and keep his way.
He will exalt you to inherit the land;
  when the wicked are destroyed, you will see it.

[35] I have seen a wicked and ruthless man
  flourishing like a luxuriant native tree,
[36] but he soon passed away and was no more;
  though I looked for him, he could not be found.

[37] Consider the blameless, observe the upright;
  a future awaits those who seek peace.
[38] But all sinners will be destroyed;
  there will be no future for the wicked.

[39] The salvation of the righteous comes from the LORD;
  he is their stronghold in time of trouble.
[40] The LORD helps them and delivers them;
  he delivers them from the wicked and saves them,
  because they take refuge in him.

David begins in verses 1-2 with the hope that evil will not stand forever. He encourages his listeners to entrust their lives to God in order to see his just deliverance (verses 3-4; 5-6; 7). He continues with a series of contrasts between the righteous and wicked (verses 8-9; 10-11; 12-13; 14-15; 16-17; 18-20; 21-22). The one who delights in Yahweh will walk upon a sure path (verses 23-24). The righteous can count on their faithfulness impacting future generations (verses 25-26). David encourages those who would turn from evil and to God's love and inheritance (verses 27-29).

At the core of the righteous one's life is the law of God (verses 30-31). David continues with a series of promises about the future security of the righteous and the perishing of the wicked (verses 32-33; 34; 35-36; 37-38). In conclusion, David reaffirms God's salvation and refuge to the righteous (verses 39-40).

As in other Psalms of David, he wrestles with what looks like the temporary and material success of the unjust and wicked people around him. He tells us that fear and envy are two emotions that can easily creep into our hearts when we wonder if there will be justice and if our cause is the right one.

Take a moment to reread the Psalm in *The Message*.

1-2 Don't bother your head with braggarts
    or wish you could succeed like the wicked.
In no time they'll shrivel like grass clippings
    and wilt like cut flowers in the sun.

3-4 Get insurance with GOD and do a good deed,
    settle down and stick to your last.
Keep company with GOD,
    get in on the best.

5-6 Open up before GOD, keep nothing back;
    he'll do whatever needs to be done:
He'll validate your life in the clear light of day
    and stamp you with approval at high noon.

7 Quiet down before GOD,
    be prayerful before him.

Don't bother with those who climb the ladder,
   who elbow their way to the top.

8-9 Bridle your anger, trash your wrath,
   cool your pipes—it only makes things worse.
Before long the crooks will be bankrupt;
   GOD-investors will soon own the store.

10-11 Before you know it, the wicked will have had it;
   you'll stare at his once famous place and—nothing!
Down-to-earth people will move in and take over,
   relishing a huge bonanza.

12-13 Bad guys have it in for the good guys,
   obsessed with doing them in.
But GOD isn't losing any sleep; to him
   they're a joke with no punch line.

14-15 Bullies brandish their swords,
   pull back on their bows with a flourish.
They're out to beat up on the harmless,
   or mug that nice man out walking his dog.
A banana peel lands them flat on their faces—
   slapstick figures in a moral circus.

16-17 Less is more and more is less.
   One righteous will outclass fifty wicked,
For the wicked are moral weaklings
   but the righteous are GOD-strong.

18-19 GOD keeps track of the decent folk;
   what they do won't soon be forgotten.
In hard times, they'll hold their heads high;
   when the shelves are bare, they'll be full.

²⁰ God-despisers have had it;
   GOD's enemies are finished —
Stripped bare like vineyards at harvest time,
   vanished like smoke in thin air.

²¹⁻²² Wicked borrows and never returns;
   Righteous gives and gives.
Generous gets it all in the end;
   Stingy is cut off at the pass.

²³⁻²⁴ Stalwart walks in step with GOD;
   his path blazed by GOD, he's happy.
If he stumbles, he's not down for long;
   GOD has a grip on his hand.

²⁵⁻²⁶ I once was young, now I'm a graybeard —
   not once have I seen an abandoned believer,
   or his kids out roaming the streets.
Every day he's out giving and lending,
   his children making him proud.

²⁷⁻²⁸ Turn your back on evil,
   work for the good and don't quit.
GOD loves this kind of thing,
   never turns away from his friends.

²⁸⁻²⁹ Live this way and you've got it made,
   but bad eggs will be tossed out.
The good get planted on good land
   and put down healthy roots.

³⁰⁻³¹ Righteous chews on wisdom like a dog on a bone,
rolls virtue around on his tongue.

His heart pumps God's Word like blood through his veins;
   his feet are as sure as a cat's.

32-33 Wicked sets a watch for Righteous,
he's out for the kill.
GOD, alert, is also on watch—
   Wicked won't hurt a hair of his head.

34 Wait passionately for GOD,
don't leave the path.
He'll give you your place in the sun
   while you watch the wicked lose it.

35-36 I saw Wicked bloated like a toad,
croaking pretentious nonsense.
The next time I looked there was nothing—
   a punctured bladder, vapid and limp.

37-38 Keep your eye on the healthy soul,
scrutinize the straight life;
There's a future
   in strenuous wholeness.
But the willful will soon be discarded;
   insolent souls are on a dead-end street.

39-40 The spacious, free life is from GOD,
it's also protected and safe.
GOD-strengthened, we're delivered from evil—
   when we run to him, he saves us.

David tells us that we can take active measures to
maintain hope when we are wondering if the wicked and
evil of the world will triumph. He uses some specific
action words to point us down the right direction. David

calls us to trust and do good; delight and commit; be still and wait; do not fret and refrain from anger. These actions help us guard against turning into the evil that we are threatened. The focus of these actions is on God himself. When our eyes get distracted by the wicked around us, David reminds us to turn our desires, emotions, ways, and vindication over to God himself.

David knows that this will be a struggle. He takes time to help us consider the eternal benefit of walking in God's good way versus the destructive way of the wicked. Taking time to look at the real difference and outcomes of the wicked and righteous life can be the best thing for us to foster hope in God. A part of this outcome is looking at the impact that our actions take on those that come behind us. How can our perseverance and hope inspire future generations when they face their own struggles?

David also points us to the firm footing found in placing the law of God in our hearts. Taking time to read, study and meditate on God's word is the key to keeping hope for the morning. This is a part of what it looks like to take refuge in God. We take his life giving word and promise and make them the bricks of the foundation of our hope.

Prayer:
God our refuge, when there is uncertainty and evil around me, it is hard from me to have hope. Help me to trust and delight in you. Give me strength to be still and wait for you to bring true justice. Give me an eternal perspective to understand what matters most. Amen.

Notes and Personal Prayer:

Psalm 59

Focus Verse:
[16] But I will sing of your strength,
in the morning I will sing of your love;
for you are my fortress,
my refuge in times of trouble.

David's early career among the leadership of Israel was anything but smooth. In 1 Samuel 19, we learn how David was forced from the strategic and honored position as the king's musician who calmed King Saul's anxious spirit to running for his life. King Saul's manic-depressant fit and spear forced David to flee for his life. Saul's henchman began a hunt for David. As David fled through the city, this Psalm reveals to us the cry of his heart to God. He looked with hope to the morning with this song of deliverance

For the director of music. To the tune of "Do Not Destroy." Of David. A *miktam*. When Saul had sent men to watch David's house in order to kill him.
[1] Deliver me from my enemies, O God;
　be my fortress against those who are attacking me.
[2] Deliver me from evildoers
　and save me from those who are after my blood.

[3] See how they lie in wait for me!
　Fierce men conspire against me
　for no offense or sin of mine, LORD.
[4] I have done no wrong, yet they are ready to attack me.
　Arise to help me; look on my plight!
[5] You, LORD God Almighty,
　you who are the God of Israel,

rouse yourself to punish all the nations;
   show no mercy to wicked traitors.

⁶ They return at evening,
   snarling like dogs,
   and prowl about the city.
⁷ See what they spew from their mouths—
   the words from their lips are sharp as swords,
   and they think, "Who can hear us?"
⁸ But you laugh at them, LORD;
   you scoff at all those nations.

⁹ You are my strength, I watch for you;
   you, God, are my fortress,
10   my God on whom I can rely.

God will go before me
   and will let me gloat over those who slander me.
¹¹ But do not kill them, Lord our shield,
   or my people will forget.
In your might uproot them
   and bring them down.
¹² For the sins of their mouths,
   for the words of their lips,
   let them be caught in their pride.
For the curses and lies they utter,
13   consume them in your wrath,
   consume them till they are no more.
Then it will be known to the ends of the earth
   that God rules over Jacob.

¹⁴ They return at evening,
   snarling like dogs,
   and prowl about the city.

¹⁵ They wander about for food
    and howl if not satisfied.
¹⁶ But I will sing of your strength,
    in the morning I will sing of your love;
for you are my fortress,
    my refuge in times of trouble.

¹⁷ You are my strength, I sing praise to you;
    you, God, are my fortress,
    my God on whom I can rely.

David begins by asking God to help him deal with Saul's blood thirst (verses 1-2). In verses 3-8, David speaks to God about Saul's conspiracies, looking for God's intervention. In the middle of the Psalm comes David's straightforward declaration of reliance on God (verses 9-10). David prays that through this, God would make his justice known among the nations (verses 10b-13). David concludes with confidence that in the morning he will be able to sing of God's deliverance (verses 14-817).

Take a moment to reread the Psalm in *The Message*.

¹⁻² My God! Rescue me from my enemies,
    defend me from these mutineers.
Rescue me from their dirty tricks,
    save me from their hit men.

³⁻⁴ Desperadoes have ganged up on me,
    they're hiding in ambush for me.
I did nothing to deserve this, GOD,
    crossed no one, wronged no one.
All the same, they're after me,
    determined to get me.

4-5 Wake up and see for yourself! You're GOD,
   GOD-of-Angel-Armies, Israel's God!
Get on the job and take care of these pagans,
   don't be soft on these hard cases.

6-7 They return when the sun goes down,
   They howl like coyotes, ringing the city.
   Then suddenly they're all at the gate,
   Snarling invective, drawn daggers in their teeth.
   They think they'll never get caught.

8-10 But you, GOD, break out laughing;
   you treat the godless nations like jokes.
Strong God, I'm watching you do it,
   I can always count on you.
God in dependable love shows up on time,
   shows me my enemies in ruin.

11-13 Don't make quick work of them, GOD,
   lest my people forget.
Bring them down in slow motion,
   take them apart piece by piece.
Let all their mean-mouthed arrogance
   catch up with them,
Catch them out and bring them down
   —every muttered curse
   —every barefaced lie.
Finish them off in fine style!
   Finish them off for good!
Then all the world will see
   that God rules well in Jacob,
   everywhere that God's in charge.

14-15 They return when the sun goes down,
    They howl like coyotes, ringing the city.
    They scavenge for bones,
    And bite the hand that feeds them.

16-17 And me? I'm singing your prowess,
    shouting at cockcrow your largesse,
For you've been a safe place for me,
    a good place to hide.
Strong God, I'm watching you do it,
    I can always count on you—
    God, my dependable love.

As David is faced with this life threatening situation (fleeing in the middle of the night from his home), he shows us a glimpse of what we can do when we feel threatened through the night hours.

First, he sees God as a reliable source of safety and strength. He says that God is his fortress (four times), shield (three times), refuge and shield. When you are evading a pursuing enemy, the one thing that you long for is a secure place. David looks to God's presence and providence as this place. This fortress is not made by the walls of a building, but the power of God.

Second, David has hope based on of the character of God. David wants the ends of the earth to know that God is faithful and just through his own situation. He looks to God with great anticipation. While his own path is uncertain, he knows God goes before him. God will consume lies and demonstrate to the nations that God is the source of truth and justice.

When we find ourselves threatened, we are called to reinforce what we know to be true. What characteristic of God do you most need to be reminded about in your situation? Write it down and repeat it to yourself regularly. This will help guard yourself in truth when surrounded by lies.

Third, we can write our song of celebration in anticipation of God's work. This may not be a song you write, but something somebody else has. Some may not think singing is for warriors, but warriors throughout history have written songs of victory. Whatever the outcome, you can look to be shielded by God's faithful and strong purpose and power. Through the uncertainties of your darkness, look to the light of morning and sing with expectation

Prayer:
God my shield and fortress, today, I keep my eyes fixed on you in these uncertain times. I ask for your character to be made known through this trial. May truth and justice prevail. Amen

Notes and Personal Prayer:

Psalm 108

Focus Verse:
[2] Awake, harp and lyre!
I will awaken the dawn.
[3] I will praise you, LORD, among the nations;
I will sing of you among the peoples.

While some may be kept up all night out of anxiety or fear, David welcomes morning with praise to God for his great love and steady faithfulness. As he looks at the threats around him, his heart comes with eager expectation in God's aid.

A song. A psalm of David.

[1] My heart, O God, is steadfast;
  I will sing and make music with all my soul.
[2] Awake, harp and lyre!
  I will awaken the dawn.
[3] I will praise you, LORD, among the nations;
  I will sing of you among the peoples.
[4] For great is your love, higher than the heavens;
  your faithfulness reaches to the skies.
[5] Be exalted, O God, above the heavens;
  let your glory be over all the earth.

[6] Save us and help us with your right hand,
  that those you love may be delivered.
[7] God has spoken from his sanctuary:
  "In triumph I will parcel out Shechem
  and measure off the Valley of Sukkoth.
[8] Gilead is mine, Manasseh is mine;
  Ephraim is my helmet,
  Judah is my scepter.
[9] Moab is my washbasin,

on Edom I toss my sandal;
over Philistia I shout in triumph."

¹⁰ Who will bring me to the fortified city?
Who will lead me to Edom?
¹¹ Is it not you, God, you who have rejected us
and no longer go out with our armies?
¹² Give us aid against the enemy,
for human help is worthless.
¹³ With God we will gain the victory,
and he will trample down our enemies.

In verses 1-5, David's heart is set on welcoming the morning with praises to God. David prays that God will aid his people and give them victory over the threatening nations around them (verses 6-9). David concludes with his complete reliance on God for victory (verses 10-13).

While surrounded by enemies, David greets the morning with praise to God. David tells us something that might aid our own expectation of each new day. First, David's prayer for help is not rooted in his own pursuit of glory or personal gain. David tells us in many ways that he wants to see God's name exalted and God's reputation honored over all the nations and among the peoples of the earth.

Second, David knows that because God is the true Lord of the nations, ultimate help and victory do not come from mere human power or persuasion. He knows that true, worthwhile help comes from God. He is the One who saves and brings true deliverance.

Take a moment to reread the Psalm in *The Message.*

¹⁻² I'm ready, God, so ready,
   ready from head to toe.
Ready to sing,
   ready to raise a God-song:
"Wake, soul! Wake, lute!
   Wake up, you sleepyhead sun!"

³⁻⁶ I'm thanking you, GOD, out in the streets,
   singing your praises in town and country.
The deeper your love, the higher it goes;
   every cloud's a flag to your faithfulness.
Soar high in the skies, O God!
   Cover the whole earth with your glory!
And for the sake of the one you love so much,
   reach down and help me—answer me!

⁷⁻⁹ That's when God spoke in holy splendor:
   "Brimming over with joy,
I make a present of Shechem,
   I hand out Succoth Valley as a gift.
Gilead's in my pocket,
   to say nothing of Manasseh.
Ephraim's my hard hat,
   Judah my hammer.
Moab's a scrub bucket—
   I mop the floor with Moab,
Spit on Edom,
   rain fireworks all over Philistia."

¹⁰⁻¹¹ Who will take me to the thick of the fight?
   Who'll show me the road to Edom?
You aren't giving up on us, are you, God?
   refusing to go out with our troops?

12-13 Give us help for the hard task;
    human help is worthless.
In God we'll do our very best;
    he'll flatten the opposition for good.

How could David's perspective help us look at the morning with hope and eager expectation?

Consider how much energy we spend on trying to bring glory to ourselves. We use much time, effort and anxiety to ensure we are seen in a positive light. Many of our fears are rooted in what people may think of us. Will we be able to prove ourselves to those who matter most to us? Even some whom may come across as humble and polite, may do so to create a self-fulfilling reputation rather than out of true sincerity. Consciously and sub-consciously this takes much mental energy, preventing our hope-filled rest. Let us ask God to give us a delight in his reputation, purpose and glory.

Think about where it is that we look for help. God can use others as a part of his way of helping us. However, when we bank our support on human help first and foremost, we will find that its worth, value and gain come up short. David calls us to look to morning with hope in the help of the One who can be surely trusted.

Prayer:
God, I worship you with eager expectation of how you will show yourself to the peoples of the world by coming to my aid. Help me to live for your honor and depend first upon your help and faithfulness. Amen.

Notes and Personal Prayer:

Psalm 143

Focus Verse:
[8] Let the morning bring me word of your unfailing love,
for I have put my trust in you.

David cries out to God in the midst of an enemy's pursuit.
He uses words like crushed, long dead, faint, dismayed
and parched to describe the situation needing God's
rescue. This most likely is during the reign of King Saul
when he violently hunted David (1 Samuel 18-31).

A psalm of David.
[1] LORD, hear my prayer,
    listen to my cry for mercy;
in your faithfulness and righteousness
    come to my relief.
[2] Do not bring your servant into judgment,
    for no one living is righteous before you.
[3] The enemy pursues me,
    he crushes me to the ground;
he makes me dwell in the darkness
    like those long dead.
[4] So my spirit grows faint within me;
    my heart within me is dismayed.
[5] I remember the days of long ago;
    I meditate on all your works
    and consider what your hands have done.
[6] I spread out my hands to you;
    I thirst for you like a parched land.

[7] Answer me quickly, LORD;
    my spirit fails.
Do not hide your face from me
    or I will be like those who go down to the pit.

⁸ Let the morning bring me word of your unfailing love,
    for I have put my trust in you.
Show me the way I should go,
    for to you I entrust my life.
⁹ Rescue me from my enemies, LORD,
    for I hide myself in you.
¹⁰ Teach me to do your will,
    for you are my God;
may your good Spirit
    lead me on level ground.

¹¹ For your name's sake, LORD, preserve my life;
    in your righteousness, bring me out of trouble.
¹² In your unfailing love, silence my enemies;
    destroy all my foes,
    for I am your servant.

In the midst of darkness, David asks for God's relief (verses 1-6). David looks for the morning light and God's rescue (verses 7-10). Through the trouble, David seeks God's unfailing love to preserve him (verses 11-12).

When we are overwhelmed in times like David's- darkness, parched and dismayed, how do we wrestle with the emotional weight? David's emotions are real and hit him hard, yet these emotions do not control his perspective or hope for the morning. David takes real action- he prays and cries for mercy. He remembers God's acts in the past and meditates on His works. He spreads out his hands, prayerfully thirsting for God's presence. He entrusts his life into God's good leading while he takes refuge in God.

On the other side of this conversation is what David asks God to do. He asks God to hear, answer and not hide. He seeks God's relief, unfailing loyalty, rescue, preservation, and victory over the enemy. In the midst of waiting, he also asks God to show him the way he should go, to teach him to do good, and to be led by God's good Spirit on a level path.

Take a moment to reread the Psalm in *The Message.*

1-2 Listen to this prayer of mine,
GOD; pay attention to what I'm asking.
   Answer me—you're famous for your answers!
      Do what's right for me.
   But don't, please don't, haul me into court;
      not a person alive would be acquitted there.

3-6 The enemy hunted me down;
      he kicked me and stomped me
      within an inch of my life.
   He put me in a black hole,
      buried me like a corpse in that dungeon.
   I sat there in despair, my spirit draining away,
      my heart heavy, like lead.
   I remembered the old days,
      went over all you've done,
      pondered the ways you've worked,
   Stretched out my hands to you,
      as thirsty for you as a desert thirsty for rain.

7-10 Hurry with your answer, GOD!
      I'm nearly at the end of my rope.
   Don't turn away; don't ignore me!

That would be certain death.
If you wake me each morning with the sound of
    your loving voice,
  I'll go to sleep each night trusting in you.
Point out the road I must travel;
  I'm all ears, all eyes before you.
Save me from my enemies, GOD—
  you're my only hope!
Teach me how to live to please you,
  because you're my God.
Lead me by your blessed Spirit
  into cleared and level pastureland.

11-12 Keep up your reputation, God—give me life!
    In your justice, get me out of this trouble!
  In your great love, vanquish my enemies;
    make a clean sweep of those who harass me.
  And why? Because I'm your servant.

How about us? When we are crushed in the midst of
darkness, how can we look to the morning light with hope
in God's unfailing love?

First, David encourages us to be aware of our emotions
but not defined by them. David was specific about his
emotions. You could look at his descriptions and see if
they relate to yours. If yours are different, what are they?
What words, colors, images, even type of music or specific
song may describe your emotions?

Next, David encourages us to find our identity not in
emotions but in God's character and reputation. We can
remember how he has worked specifically in our lives, in
our family and friends' lives. We can look in history both

biblical and modern history. This may take some time to read and to talk to others. We can do more than remember, we can meditate and considers God's works. This means wrestling with what those works mean; what they taught; what they tell us about God's character; and how they could be repeated in our own situation.

Lastly, in the midst of waiting on God's timing, we need a path through the darkness and trouble. When we pray to God, we should be specific about the situation or relationships that we need a clear and level path to walk and engage. We should seek God's will, not just our emotional response. Often God's will is less about changing our circumstances and more about forming our character as we learn to trust in His.

Prayer:
Rescuing and relieving God, you have brought your people out of darkness and into the light of your unfailing love. Today, while my emotions are real and a part of how I am reacting to this situation, help me to also fix my eyes on your ways and your wisdom. Teach and show me how to navigate through this darkness and into the morning light of your love. Amen.

Notes and Personal Prayer

A SHORT BIOGRAPHY OF KING DAVID

David was from Bethlehem in Judah and the youngest of eight sons of Jesse from the tribe of Judah. His youth was spent serving his family as a shepherd in the countryside of Judah. As a shepherd he learned of God's strength when he defeated a lion and bear who attacked the flock (1 Samuel 17:34-35).

It was while David was working as a shepherd that God sent the prophet Samuel to anoint him as the next shepherd-king of Israel (1 Samuel 16:1-13). David continued working for his father; however, "the Spirit of the Lord came upon David from that day forward," and "the Spirit of the Lord departed from Saul" (1 Samuel 16:13-14). From that point on, King Saul struggled with a troubled spirit. Ironically, David was requested for his musical ability to play the harp to sooth Saul's depressed state (1 Samuel 16:14-23).

After returning home, David was called again into the service of King Saul. Jesse sent David to resupply his brothers, who were fighting under King Saul against the Philistines. The battle had come to a standstill because Israel was intimidated by Goliath, the Philistines' giant war champion. David would not stand for Goliath's attacks against Israel's God. He requested that King Saul allow him to take up Goliath's challenge in a dual. God gave David (the underdog) victory over this giant when he killed him with the stone from his sling and cut off his head (1 Samuel 17).

David's victory made him a national hero. Saul gave David his daughter Michal in marriage, but King Saul developed a dangerous jealousy toward David's victories (1 Samuel 18:6-16). King Saul grew to violently hate David and caused David to flee as a fugitive (1 Samuel 18-30). However, God used David's friendship with Jonathan, Saul's son, to aid David in the midst of these plots. David fled to Samuel and other prophets at Ramah (1 Samuel 19:12-18). Some think that Psalms 6, 7 and 11 were composed by him at this time. Eventually, David had to flee Saul again. First, he went to Nob (1 Samuel 21:1-9) and then at Gath, the capital city of the Philistines. The Philistine king did not trust David, so David went on to the stronghold of Adullam (1 Samuel 22:1-4; 1 Chronicles 12:8-18). Soon, some 400 warriors came to him and entrusted themselves to his leadership (1 Samuel 22:1-2). Latter he moved into the forest of Hereth (1 Samuel 22:5).

Once, Saul heard about David's movements, he gave orders for the massacre of the entire priestly family at Nob. This devastating news was brought to David by Abiathar, son of Ahimelech, the only survivor (2 Samuel 22:6-23). David's response to this awful news is found in Psalm 52.

David and his men went to the aid of the town of Keilah when they were harassed by the Philistines (1 Samuel 23:1-14). Because of Saul's pursuit, they fled to the hill country of Judah. David's reflection on this is in Psalm 31. There, Jonathan visited David for the last time and encouraged him to persevere (1 Samuel 23:16-18). Again, to avoid King Saul, they maneuvered the crags and ravines of Engedi, on the western shore of the Dead Sea (1 Samuel 23:29). King Saul continued to pursue him with his army. However, Saul narrowly escaped death because David refused to kill God's anointed king before his appointed time (1 Samuel 24).

David moved with his now 600 men to Maon, where they lived off the contributions gathered from the people of the district. When one of the region's power brokers would not aid David and his men after they protected his flocks, David nearly slaughtered Nabal's entire house. However, the strategic intervention of Nabal's wife, Abigail kept him from it. After, God struck down Nabal for his pride, David married Abigail (1 Samuel 25).

Again, David was pursued by King Saul in the wilderness of Ziph (1 Samuel 26). Again, David had opportunity slay King Saul but would not touch God's anointed before his time. Eventfully, David was given refuge among the Philistines in the city of Ziglag (1 Samuel 27). David lived there with his men and their families. They engaged in frequent skirmishes with the Amalekites and other tribes on the south of Judah. When Ziklag was raided and families kidnapped while David and his men were out on mission, David and his men pursued the Amalekites raiders. David completely defeated them and rescued their families.

On his return to Ziklag, David received word of Saul and Jonathan's death in combat near Mount Gilboa (2 Samuel 1). An Amalekite brought Saul's crown and bracelet and laid them at his feet. David and his men mourned for King Saul and Jonathan. David wrote a hymn of tribute to Saul and Jonathan (2 Samuel 1:18-27).

God sent David and his men to Hebron where he was anointed as king over Judah (2 Samuel 2:1-4). However, his rule over all of Israel was disputed. Civil war broke out when Ish-bosheth, Saul's only remaining son was crowned king. David and his trusted military leader, Joab eventually won the day, and the opposition was put down (2 Samuel 2-4). The elders of Israel came to Hebron to give allegiance to David (2 Samuel 5:1-5). Once anointed king of all Israel, he established his capital in the Jebusite fortress on Mount Zion, later named Jerusalem (2 Samuel 5:6-15). Twice the Philistines challenged David's kingship but where routed as God aided David and his armies. (2 Samuel 5:17-25).

Once David had established his kingdom, he desired to bring the Ark of the Covenant to Jerusalem (2 Samuel 6). David led the procession of worship into Jerusalem with the Ark of the Covenant. Psalm 24 is possibly a psalm he wrote for this joyous occasion. David established a tent-like tabernacle for the ark and for the worship of God (1 Chronicles 16). David felt compelled to build a temple for the ark of God. While God would not have David build a temple because his role was of a warrior-king not temple builder, God would make David's descendents great, allowing his son Solomon to build the temple and eventually one who would be an eternal king (2 Samuel 7:1-16). David also greatly expanded the territory of Israel from the Euphrates to the Nile and from Gaza on the west to Thapsacus on the east (2 Samuel 8:3-13; 10).

At the height of his glory, David committed the sin of adultery and murder (2 Samuel 11). While his military triumphs are recorded in a few verses, the sad story of his fall is given in detail. It was Nathan the prophet who God sent to confront David of his crimes (2 Samuel 7:1-17; 12:1-23). Psalm 32 and 51 reveal David's contrition and his spiritual recovery. While Bathsheba became his wife after Uriah's murder, their first-born son died, as Nathan foretold. Their second son was Solomon, who ultimately succeeded David on the throne (2 Samuel 12:24-25).

David's reign again experienced times of distress. His eldest son Amnon raped his half-sister Tamar (2 Samuel 13). After two years, the second son, Absalom terribly avenged the crime against Tamar and murdered Amnon. Absalom fled for three years, breaking his relationship with his father. Absalom took advantage of national weakness and attempted to rally the people to him. His followers crowned him king at Hebron, and forced David to abandon Jerusalem like a fugitive (2 Samuel 15:13-20). A civil war broke out, leading to the defeat of Absalom and his army. David was able to return to Jerusalem.

Then a dispute arose between the men of Judah and the men of Israel (2 Samuel 19:41-43). Sheba, a Benjamite, led a revolt of the men of Israel. This revolt also eventually was put down (2 Samuel 20). Then there came three years of famine (2 Samuel. 21:1-14). Next, pestilence came as a punishment for David's pride in numbering the people. At least 70,000 died throughout Israel(2 Samuel 24).

After the rebellions and distress, David experienced ten mostly peaceful years. He spent this time gathering resources of every kind for the great temple at Jerusalem, which God promised his successor would build (1 Chronicles 22; 28; 29).

As David drew closer to death, a quarrel broke out as to who should be his successor. David's top military leader, Joab favored Adonijah. Nathan, the prophet waited for

David's decision in favor of Solomon. Solomon was brought to Jerusalem and was anointed king on his father's throne (1 Kings 1:11-53). David's last words reveal his deep faith in God and his joyful confidence in God's promises (2 Samuel 23:1-7). David reigned forty years and six months and died at the age of seventy years, "and was buried in the city of David" on Mount Zion (2 Samuel 5:5; 1 Chronicles 3:4; around B.C. 1015).

THE PSALMS WRITTEN BY DAVID

There are fourteen psalms that were written by David to commemorate important events in his life. Some have been covered in the preceding reflections. You could use the following list to guide your own study of the rest of King David's Psalms. The following list and descriptions are from

http://www.lwbc.co.uk/davids_psalms.htm

Psalm 59
King Saul, in his jealousy, sent messengers to David's house to kill him, but he was able to escape before the men could enter. David's wife Michal (Saul's daughter) was able to deceive the men while David made his way to safety (1 Samuel 19).

Psalm 56
This psalm was written by David when he went to live in Gath (in Philistine territory). He pretended to be mad so that he might be allowed into the city. David did this because he was afraid and thought that he would be safe amongst the Philistines. His act must have been believable

since Achish would not let such a madman live in his city (1 Samuel 21:10-15). The psalm expresses both his fear of man and his faith in God.

Psalm 34
This was written for the same occasion as mentioned above (1 Samuel 21:10-15). David praises God for His goodness despite the fact that he had to flee his wife and home. His faith told him that God would deliver him from all his enemies.

Psalm 142
After being cast out by Achish, David fled to a cave in Adullam (1 Samuel 22:1-3). He was overwhelmed because of the desperate situation he was in. He was obviously lonely, but he found refuge in the Lord. He felt that this cave was a prison to him.

Psalm 63
David fled from Saul into the Judean wilderness (1 Samuel 22:5). In the psalm he sees himself in a spiritual wilderness, thirsting for God's presence and a place of refuge.

Psalm 52
David heard how Saul had sent Doeg the Edomite to Ahimelech's house and slew eighty-five priests, including their wives, children, and animals. David was heartbroken over such wickedness (1 Samuel 22:9-19).

Psalm 54
The Ziphites went to Saul and told him that David was hiding amongst them. They told him exactly where they

could locate David (1 Samuel 23:19-29), but God delivered him out of the king's hands.

Psalm 57
Saul went after David again when he heard that he was hiding in the wilderness of Engedi. Saul entered a cave to relieve himself, the very cave where David and his men were hiding. David managed to get close enough to Saul to cut off a piece of his cloak. David revealed to the king that he would have killed him if he had wanted to. David proved that he was more merciful that Saul (1 Samuel 24:1-22).

Psalm 7
Cush the Benjaminite had been feeding Saul with lies about David. He told Saul that David had been seeking to kill him all along (1 Samuel 24:9-12). In this psalm, David reveals that he freed him that was his enemy rather than seeking to destroy him. He prays that the mischief of Cush return upon his own head.

Psalm 60
This was written to commemorate David's victory over the Philistines, Moabites, and the Syrians (2 Samuel 8; 1 Kings 11). David praises God for the great victory.

Psalm 51
This is probably one of the best known of David's songs and there is little difficulty in placing it within the context of his life. In 2 Samuel 12, we read of David's sin of adultery with Bathsheba the wife of Uriah the Hittite. Not only did he commit adultery, but he also arranged the murder of Uriah. It was only when the prophet Nathan

rebuked him that David repented of his wickedness. This psalm expresses his deep sorrow over his sin. Psalm 32 may be part of this repentance also.

Psalm 3

Absalom, David's son, sought to take the kingdom from him. He was very successful in persuading the people that he would make a better king than his father. Because of his son's success he was forced to flee Jerusalem (2 Samuel 15). This psalm is David's lament over this situation.

Psalm 30

Written to commemorate the plans for the building of the Temple in Jerusalem and dedication of the site (1 Chronicles 22). He is both thankful to God for freeing him from all his enemies, the forgiveness of sin of numbering his people, and the privilege of laying plans for a house for the Lord.

LIST OF PSALMS WRITTEN BY DAVID

There are seventy-three Psalms written by David.

Psalm 3 Confidence facing the enemy

Psalm 4 Thoughts in the night

Psalm 5 A morning prayer

Psalm 6 Prayer for mercy during trouble

Psalm 7 The prayer of a wronged man

Psalm 8 God's glory and man's honor

Psalm 9 Praise for deliverance

Psalm 11 God our refuge

Psalm 12 Good thoughts for bad times

Psalm 13 The deserted soul

Psalm 14 The future of the fool

Psalm 15 The happiness of the holy

Psalm 16 Joy in God's presence

Psalm 17 Deliverance from the wicked

Psalm 18 Calling upon God in distress

Psalm 19 The works and word of God

Psalm 20 A prayer for the king

Psalm 21 Splendor and success of the king

Psalm 22 Psalm of the Cross / Hind of the morning

Psalm 23 The Shepherd Psalm

Psalm 24 Song to the King of Glory

Psalm 25 Prayer for guidance and protection

Psalm 26 The basis of judgment

Psalm 27 David's song of confidence

Psalm 28 A prayer for help

Psalm 29 Song of the thunderstorm

Psalm 30 Dedication of the temple site

Psalm 31 My times are in Thy hands

Psalm 32 A prayer during distress

Psalm 34 A psalm of praise and trust

Psalm 35 A plea for judgment

Psalm 36 Wickedness confronts God's love
Psalm 37 Blessings to the righteous
Psalm 38 The burden of suffering
Psalm 39 In time of trouble
Psalm 40 Delight in the will of God
Psalm 41 Psalm of the compassionate
Psalm 51 The Penitent's Psalm
Psalm 52 The fate of the wicked
Psalm 53 The fate of the fool
Psalm 54 A prayer for deliverance
Psalm 55 The Lord will sustain
Psalm 56 A song for the distressed
Psalm 57 The mercy and truth of God
Psalm 58 The punishment of the wicked
Psalm 59 Triumph over enemies
Psalm 60 Prayer for national deliverance
Psalm 61 The prayer of a troubled heart
Psalm 62 Confidence in God
Psalm 63 The thirsty soul
Psalm 64 Appeal for help against enemies
Psalm 65 God's provisions for the earth
Psalm 66 God's power and works
Psalm 68 The God of Israel
Psalm 69 The prayer for deliverance
Psalm 70 Deliverance from persecutors
Psalm 86 Prayer for deliverance
Psalm 101 A perfect heart
Psalm 103 The benefits of the Lord
Psalm 108 A song of confidence in God
Psalm 109 A cry to God for help
Psalm 110 The king as priest and victor
Psalm 122 The peace of Jerusalem
Psalm 124 God's deliverance
Psalm 131 A song of the humble

Psalm 138 The Lord is faithful
Psalm 139 The prayer of a believing heart
Psalm 140 For protection against enemies
Psalm 141 Conduct amidst trials
Psalm 142 The prisoner's prayer
Psalm 143 The prayer of the soul in distress
Psalm 144 The warrior's psalm
Psalm 145 The goodness of the Lord

OTHER PSALMS DEALING WITH
SLEEP AND REST

Psalm 1
Psalm 16
Psalm 42
Psalm 49
Psalm 59
Psalm 74
Psalm 77
Psalm 88
Psalm 90
Psalm 91
Psalm 92
Psalm 107
Psalm 112
Psalm 116
Psalm 119
Psalm 121
Psalm 127
Psalm 130
Psalm 134
Psalm 149

HELPFUL BOOKS ON THE PSALMS

Lawson, Steven and Max Anders. *Holman Old Testament Commentary - Psalms.*

Longman, **Tremper.** *How to Read the Psalms.*

Longman, **Tremper.** *Psalms (The Expositor's Bible Commentary).*

Peterson, **Eugene H.** *Answering God: The Psalms as Tools for Prayer.*

Peterson, **Eugene H.** *Praying with the Psalms: A Year of Daily Prayers and Reflections on the Words of David.*

Peterson, **Eugene H.** *The Message The Book of Psalms.*

Reardon, **Patrick Henry.** *Christ in the Psalms.*

Sire, **James W.** *Learning to Pray Through the Psalms.*

Webster, Brian and **David R. Beach.** *The Essential Bible Companion to the Psalms: Key Insights for Reading God's Word (Essential Bible Companion Series).*

For more information on reading the Bible and knowing God's ultimate warrior- Jesus the Messiah, go to:
http://www.biblica.com/living-the-script/

For Bible Reading Plans and other Bible Resources:
http://www.biblegateway.com/

SLEEP RESOURCES

SLEEP DISORDERS
http://www.cdc.gov/sleep/about_sleep/key_disorders.htm

Sleep-related difficulties affect many people. The following is a description of some of the major sleep disorders. If you, or someone you know, is experiencing any of the following, it is important to receive an evaluation by a healthcare provider or, if necessary, a provider specializing in sleep medicine.

Insomnia
Insomnia is characterized by an inability to initiate or maintain sleep. It may also take the form of *early morning awakening* in which the individual awakens several hours early and is unable to resume sleeping. Difficulty initiating or maintaining sleep may often manifest itself as *excessive daytime sleepiness*, which characteristically results in functional impairment throughout the day. Before arriving at a diagnosis of primary insomnia, the healthcare provider will rule out other potential causes, such as other sleep disorders, side effects of medications, substance abuse, depression, or other previously undetected illness. *Chronic psychophysiological insomnia* (or "learned" or "conditioned" insomnia) may result from a stressor combined with fear of being unable to sleep. Individuals with this condition may sleep better when not in their own beds. Health care providers may treat chronic insomnia with a combination of use of sedative-hypnotic or sedating antidepressant medications, along with behavioral techniques to promote regular sleep.

Narcolepsy

Excessive daytime sleepiness (including episodes of *irresistible sleepiness*) combined with sudden muscle weakness are the hallmark signs of narcolepsy. The sudden muscle weakness seen in narcolepsy may be elicited by strong emotion or surprise. Episodes of narcolepsy have been described as "sleep attacks" and may occur in unusual circumstances, such as walking and other forms of physical activity. The healthcare provider may treat narcolepsy with stimulant medications combined with behavioral interventions, such as regularly scheduled naps, to minimize the potential disruptiveness of narcolepsy on the individual's life.

Restless Legs Syndrome (RLS)

RLS is characterized by an unpleasant "creeping" sensation, often feeling like it is originating in the lower legs, but often associated with aches and pains throughout the legs. This often causes difficulty initiating sleep and is relieved by movement of the leg, such as walking or kicking. Abnormalities in the neurotransmitter *dopamine* have often been associated with RLS. Healthcare providers often combine a medication to help correct the underlying dopamine abnormality along with a medicine to promote sleep continuity in the treatment of RLS.

Sleep Apnea

Snoring may be more than just an annoying habit – it may be a sign of sleep apnea. Persons with sleep apnea characteristically make periodic gasping or "snorting" noises, during which their sleep is momentarily interrupted. Those with sleep apnea may also experience excessive daytime sleepiness, as their sleep is commonly interrupted and may not feel restorative. Treatment of sleep apnea is dependent on its cause. If other medical problems are present, such as *congestive heart failure* or nasal obstruction, sleep apnea may resolve with treatment of these conditions. Gentle air pressure administered during sleep (typically in the form of a nasal *continuous positive airway pressure* device) may also be effective in the treatment of sleep apnea. As interruption of regular breathing or obstruction of the airway during sleep can pose serious health complications, symptoms of sleep apnea should be taken seriously. Treatment should be sought from a health care provider.

SLEEP EVALUATION

The following information comes from Nancy Foldvary-Schaefer, *The Cleveland Clinic Guide to Sleep Disorders.* New York: Kaplan Publishers, 2009.

What we know about sleep: (page 6)

- Sleep needs are genetically determined; most bodies need more than six hours.
- We can't learn to sleep less; it is a biological necessity to operate with a full capacity.
- Sleep is not a waste of time.
- Sleepiness is not a character flaw necessarily; it is either sleep deprivation or a sleep disorder.

How Do I Know If I Have A Sleep Disorder? (page 16-17)

These are some basic questions to ask yourself to evaluate if you need to seek additional assistance with your sleep. If you answer yes to any of these, there is a need for you to seek assistance with either sleep hygiene or monitoring and treatment.

- Are you often tired or sleepy during the day?
- Do you snore or is your breathing interrupted during sleep?
- Do you kick or thrash while you sleep?
- Do you have trouble falling or staying a sleep?
- Do you have a family history of sleep disorders?
- Do you have an urge to move your legs at night that interferes with your ability to fall asleep?
- Do you experience unusual behaviors while you sleep, such as walking, eating, or acting out dreams that interfere with sleep quality or have caused injury to yourself or others?

- Do you have irregular or inconsistent sleep and wake-up times? Is your bedroom environment noisy, bright, or uncomfortable?
- Has your sleep problem been present for more than three months?

Sleep Deprivation Signals (page 18)

The following are signs of sleep deprivation. If you have suffered from the following, you may want to seek assistance from a doctor and/or a sleep specialist.

- Impaired memory or shortened attention span
- Loss of temper or irritability
- Dozing off or head nodding while you are driving a car or attending a meeting.
- Hitting the alarm clock snooze button repeatedly.
- Feeling unmotivated or lacking energy to "get going."

Fatigue Severity Scale (page 26-27)

In this scale, choose a number between 1-7 for each questions (1= strongly disagree; 7 = strongly agree). This will measure the impact of fatigue on how you function.

- My motivation is lower when I am fatigued.
- Exercise brings on my fatigue.
- I am easily fatigued.
- Fatigue interferes with my physical conditioning.
- Fatigue causes frequent problems for me.
- My fatigue prevents sustained physical functioning.
- My fatigue interferes with carrying out certain duties and responsibilities.
- Fatigue is among my three most disabling symptoms.

- Fatigue interferes with my work, family or social life.

The total should range from 9-63. A score of 36 or higher is abnormal. This indicates a significant functional impairment due to fatigue.

SLEEP JOURNAL
http://www.cdc.gov/sleep/about_sleep/cant_sleep.htm

It's important to practice good sleep hygiene, but if your sleep problems persist or if they interfere with how you feel or function during the day, you should seek evaluation and treatment by a physician, preferably one familiar with assessing and treating sleep disorders. Before visiting your physician, keep a diary of your sleep habits for about ten days to discuss at the visit.

Include the following in your sleep diary, when you—

- Go to bed.
- Go to sleep.
- Wake up.
- Get out of bed.
- Take naps.
- Exercise.
- Consume alcohol.
- Consume caffeinated beverages.

SLEEP HYGIENE
http://healthysleep.med.harvard.edu/healthy/getting/overcoming/tips

Twelve Simple Tips to Improve Your Sleep

Falling asleep may seem like an impossible dream when you're awake at 3 a.m., but good sleep is more under your control than you might think. Following healthy sleep habits can make the difference between restlessness and restful slumber. Researchers have identified a variety of practices and habits—known as "sleep hygiene"—that can help anyone maximize the hours they spend sleeping, even those whose sleep is affected by insomnia, jet lag, or shift work.

Sleep hygiene may sound unimaginative, but it just may be the best way to get the sleep you need in this 24/7 age. Here are some simple tips for making the sleep of your dreams a nightly reality:

#1 Avoid Caffeine, Alcohol, Nicotine, and Other Chemicals that Interfere with Sleep

Caffeinated products decrease a person's quality of sleep. As any coffee lover knows, caffeine is a stimulant that can keep you awake. So avoid caffeine (found in coffee, tea, chocolate, cola, and some pain relievers) for four to six hours before bedtime. Similarly, smokers should refrain from using tobacco products too close to bedtime

Although alcohol may help bring on sleep, after a few hours it acts as a stimulant, increasing the number of awakenings and generally decreasing the quality of sleep later in the night. It is therefore best to limit alcohol consumption to one to two drinks per day, or less, and to avoid drinking within three hours of bedtime.

#2 Turn Your Bedroom into a Sleep-Inducing Environment

A quiet, dark, and cool environment can help promote sound slumber. Why do you think bats congregate in caves for their daytime sleep? To achieve such an environment, lower the volume of outside noise with earplugs or a "white noise" appliance. Use heavy curtains, blackout shades, or an eye mask to block light, a powerful cue that tells the brain that it's time to wake up. Keep the temperature comfortably cool—between 60 and 75°F—and the room well ventilated. And make sure your bedroom is equipped with a comfortable mattress and pillows. (Remember that most mattresses wear out after ten years.)

Also, if a pet regularly wakes you during the night, you may want to consider keeping it out of your bedroom.

It may help to limit your bedroom activities to sleep and sex only. Keeping computers, TVs, and work materials out of the room will strengthen the mental association between your bedroom and sleep.

#3 Establish a Soothing Pre-Sleep Routine

Ease the transition from wake time to sleep time with a period of relaxing activities an hour or so before bed. Take a bath (the rise, then fall in body temperature promotes drowsiness), read a book, watch television, or practice relaxation exercises. Avoid stressful, stimulating activities—doing work, discussing emotional issues. Physically and psychologically stressful activities can cause the body to secrete the stress hormone cortisol, which is associated with increasing alertness. If you tend

to take your problems to bed, try writing them down—
and then putting them aside.

#4 Go to Sleep When You're Truly Tired
Struggling to fall sleep just leads to frustration. If you're
not asleep after 20 minutes, get out of bed, go to another
room, and do something relaxing, like reading or listening
to music until you are tired enough to sleep.

#5 Don't Be a Nighttime Clock-Watcher
Staring at a clock in your bedroom, either when you are
trying to fall asleep or when you wake in the middle of the
night, can actually increase stress, making it harder to fall
asleep. Turn your clock's face away from you.

And if you wake up in the middle of the night and can't
get back to sleep in about 20 minutes, get up and engage
in a quiet, restful activity such as reading or listening to
music. And keep the lights dim; bright light can stimulate
your internal clock. When your eyelids are drooping and
you are ready to sleep, return to bed.

#6 Use Light to Your Advantage
Natural light keeps your internal clock on a healthy sleep-
wake cycle. So let in the light first thing in the morning
and get out of the office for a sun break during the day.

#7 Keep Your Internal Clock Set with a Consistent Sleep Schedule
Going to bed and waking up at the same time each day
sets the body's "internal clock" to expect sleep at a certain
time night after night. Try to stick as closely as possible to
your routine on weekends to avoid a Monday morning
sleep hangover. Waking up at the same time each day is

the very best way to set your clock, and even if you did not sleep well the night before, the extra sleep drive will help you consolidate sleep the following night.

#8 Nap Early—Or Not at All

Many people make naps a regular part of their day. However, for those who find falling asleep or staying asleep through the night problematic, afternoon napping may be one of the culprits. This is because late-day naps decrease sleep drive. If you must nap, it's better to keep it short and before 5 p.m.

#9 Lighten Up on Evening Meals

Eating a pepperoni pizza at 10 p.m. may be a recipe for insomnia. Finish dinner several hours before bedtime and avoid foods that cause indigestion. If you get hungry at night, snack on foods that (in your experience) won't disturb your sleep, perhaps dairy foods and carbohydrates.

#10 Balance Fluid Intake

Drink enough fluid at night to keep from waking up thirsty—but not so much and so close to bedtime that you will be awakened by the need for a trip to the bathroom.

#11 Exercise Early

Exercise can help you fall asleep faster and sleep more soundly—as long as it's done at the right time. Exercise stimulates the body to secrete the stress hormone cortisol, which helps activate the alerting mechanism in the brain. This is fine, unless you're trying to fall asleep. Try to finish exercising at least three hours before bed or work out earlier in the day.

#12 Follow Through

Some of these tips will be easier to include in your daily and nightly routine than others. However, if you stick with them, your chances of achieving restful sleep will improve. That said, not all sleep problems are so easily treated and could signify the presence of a sleep disorder such as apnea, restless legs syndrome, narcolepsy, or another clinical sleep problem. If your sleep difficulties don't improve through good sleep hygiene, you may want to consult your physician or a sleep specialist.

SLEEP WEBSITES

https://sleep.med.harvard.edu/what-we-do/public-education
http://healthysleep.med.harvard.edu/portal/

http://stanfordhospital.org/clinicsmedServices/clinics/sleep/

http://www.sleepfoundation.org/
http://www.sleepfoundation.org/sleep-facts-information/sleeping-smart
http://www.sleepfoundation.org/article/how-sleep-works/what-happens-when-you-sleep
http://www.sleepfoundation.org/article/hot-topics/five-clusters-sleep-patterns
http://www.sleepfoundation.org/article/hot-topics/sleeping-when-it-blistering-hot
http://www.sleepfoundation.org/article/sleep-topics/food-and-sleep
http://www.sleepfoundation.org/article/sleep-topics/jet-lag-and-sleep
http://www.sleepfoundation.org/sleep-facts-information/myths-and-facts

http://www.sleepassociation.org
http://www.sleepassociation.org/index.php?p=sleephygienetips

Notes and Personal Prayers

Notes and Personal Prayers

Made in the USA
Columbia, SC
16 August 2025

61446294R10089